Speech Prosody in
Atypical Populations

Speech Prosody in Atypical Populations

Assessment and Remediation

Vesna Stojanovik and Jane Setter (Eds)

J&R Press Ltd

© 2011 J&R Press Ltd

Library of Congress Cataloguing in Publication Data

British Library Cataloguing in Publication Data

A catalogue record for this book is available from the British Library

Cover design: Jim Wilkie

Project management, typesetting and design: J&R Publishing Services Ltd, Guildford, Surrey, UK; www.jr-publishingservices.co.uk

Images reproduced on page 98 by permission of Shutterstock.com:
posed by models

Printed and bound in Great Britain by
CPI Antony Rowe, Chippenham and Eastbourne

Contents

About the Authors

Evelyn Abberton is a phonetician and Fellow of the Royal College of Speech and Language Therapists. She has a special research interest in inter-disciplinary work characterizing normal and pathological voice quality, an area in which she has been active as a member of European consortia, and as supervisor of research students. For many years she taught and examined undergraduate and postgraduate students of Speech and Language Therapy at University College London where she is currently an Honorary Senior Research Fellow in the Department of Speech, Hearing and Phonetic Sciences.

Jan Anward is Professor of Language and Culture and director of the Graduate School in Language and Culture in Europe at the Department of Culture and Communication, Linköping University, Sweden. His main research interest is language as a dynamic, co-constructed, and distributed system, and the implications of this view of language for speech therapy and education. He is the author of *Språkbruk och språkutveckling I skolan* (1983) and numerous scholarly articles, and the editor, with Bengt Nordberg, of *Samtal och grammatik* (2005).

Suzanne Beeke is a speech and language therapist, Senior Lecturer and Head of the Research Department of Language and Communication at University College London. Her main research interest involves the application of conversation analysis to the study of communication disorders, particularly aphasia, but also dysarthria and dementia. She has written about grammar and prosody as adaptive resources in the conversations of speakers with Broca's aphasia. She is currently evaluating a novel conversation-based therapy for people with agrammatic aphasia.

Adrian Fourcin is an Emeritus Professor at University College London. His major interests are in the areas of voice: perception, production and analysis. This has led to work on: neural mechanisms of pitch perception, voice pattern hearing aids for the deaf, speech development, speech technology and, particularly, the investigation and introduction of Laryngograph®-based methods for normal and pathological voice measurement and biofeedback. He is the recipient of the Voice Foundation of America's Quintana Award for Voice Research and of the International Speech Communication's Outstanding Speech Scientist Award.

Deborah Kelly is a lead speech and language therapist working in special schools in Warwickshire. Her research arose from work in mainstream schools during her study for the MSc Human Communication at University College London. She continues to use video extensively in her work with both parents and children as a means of illustrating behaviours and monitoring change.

Peter Mariën obtained a Master's degree in Linguistics at the University of Antwerp (Belgium). He then studied Neurolinguistics at the Vrije Universiteit Brussels. As a clinical neurolinguist in the department of Neurology of ZNA AZ Middelheim hospital in Antwerp he obtained his PhD in 2001 in the Faculty of Medicine of the University of Antwerp under the supervision of Professor Peter P. De Deyn (Antwerp) and Professor Luigi A. Vignolo (Brescia, Italy) with a doctoral thesis entitled 'The Lateralized Linguistic Brain: A study on crossed aphasia in dextrals'. In addtition to his clinical work at ZNA AZ Middelheim hospital in Antwerp, he is affiliated as Professor in Neurolinguistics with the Vrije Universiteit Brussels (Faculty of Arts) and University of Ghent (Faculty of Medicine). Peter Mariën's main area of research is situated in the field of clinical neurolinguistics and clinical neuropsychology (e.g., neurological speech and language disorders, cerebellar neurocognition).

Ulrika Nettelbladt is a Professor in Logopedics (Speech-Language Therapy) at Lund University, Sweden. She took her PhD in Phonetics in 1983 and has also a professional background as a certified speech-language therapist. Her early research and published work have focused on phonological, especially prosodic and phonotactic aspects, in Swedish children with language impairment. She has also been involved in cross-linguistic research concerning phonological and grammatical impairment in children. More recent research interests cover interaction and intervention and also the history of Logopedics. She is currently involved in research in bilingual children with language impairment with a particular focus on lexical and pragmatic aspects of development.

Sue Peppé has specialized for 20 years in the assessment of prosody and intonation in communication disorders. Following her MA at University College London she spent several years working there on intonation in the Survey of English Usage with Randolph Quirk and others. She then devised the procedure 'Profiling Elements of Prosody in Speech-Communication' ('PEPS-C') with Dr Bill Wells and Joanne Cleland, and was awarded a doctorate in Speech Sciences in 1998 for a thesis entitled 'Investigating linguistic prosodic ability in adult speakers of English'. This test, available in French, Spanish, Flemish, Norwegian and five versions for English regional accents, has been used in several publicly-funded studies of prosody in adults and children. For the last 10 years she has been a Research Fellow at Queen Margaret University, Edinburgh, specializing in prosody in autism.

Charlotta Plejert holds a PhD in Linguistics and is a Senior Lecturer at the Department of Culture and Communication, Linköping University, Sweden. Her research and writing is on conversation analysis, second language acquisition and language impairment in children and adults. She is currently involved in two major research projects funded by the Swedish Tercentary Foundation (RJ) and the Swedish Research Council (VR). Previous and current research deal with co-construction of understanding in interaction involving people with a communicative impairment in institutional as well as everyday settings. She is editor, together with Christina Samuelsson and Niklas Norén, of the book *Aided Communication in Everyday Interaction* (J&R Press Ltd, 2012). She is also reviewer for *System*.

Christina Samuelsson has a PhD in Medical Sciences, is a speech language pathologist and is a Senior Lecturer at the Department of Neuroscience and Locomotion, Division of Speech Language Pathology, Linköping University, Sweden. Her academic writings are on language impairment in children and adults, prosody, interaction and pragmatics. Her main research interest is prosody, and its relationship to various types of communication disabilities, such as language impairment in children and aphasia in adults. In addition to this, she is also involved in research related to language and cognitive development in children with hearing loss and different types of hearing aids, e.g., cochlear implants. Another interest is the development of the use of conversation analysis as a method in various fields of speech and language pathology, both in research and in clinical work. Together with Charlotta Plejert and Niklas Norén she is editor of *Aided Communication in Everyday Interaction* (J&R Press Ltd, 2012).

Jane Setter is Senior Lecturer in Phonetics at the University of Reading, UK, Department of English Language and Literature. She holds a PhD in Phonetics from Reading, and MA and BA degrees from the University of Leeds, UK. Jane's research interests are in the phonology of new and emergent varieties of English, English phonetics and phonology, and prosodic features of atypical speech; she is co-author of *Hong Kong English* (Edinburgh University Press, 2010), co-editor of the *Cambridge English Pronouncing Dictionary* (17th edition, Cambridge University Press, 2006), has been invited speaker at several international conferences, and has published in successful partnership with Vesna Stojanovik on speech prosody in Williams syndrome. Jane also acts as an examiner on the International Phonetic Association's Certificate of Proficiency in the Phonetics of English.

Vesna Stojanovik is a Senior Lecturer in Clinical Linguistics in the School of Psychology and Clinical Language Sciences at the University of Reading. She holds a BA in English Language and Literature and French Language and Literature from the University of Ss Cyril and Methodius, Skopje, Macedonia, an MA in Linguistics and English Language Teaching from the University of Leeds, and a PhD in Human Communication Sciences from the University of Sheffield. Her main research interests include speech, language and communication disorders in atypical populations, particularly children affected by genetic syndromes such as Williams and Down's syndrome.

Gwen Van Nuffelen is a speech and language pathologist at the Antwerp University Hospital, with substantial experience in voice disorders, dysarthria and dysphagia and is a member of the Motor Speech Committee of the International Association of Logopedics and Phoniatrics. This specific interest mirrors in her scientific work. In 2009 she finished her PhD research on speech intelligibility in dysarthria. Nowadays, her main research interests involve speech production in dysarthria – with special interest for intelligibility and prosody – and dysphagia.

Jo Verhoeven studied General Linguistics at the University of Antwerp from which he graduated in 1981. From there, he went on to study Neurolinguistics at the Vrije Universiteit Brussels and Phonetics at the University of Edinburgh where he obtained a Master of Science in Phonetics in 1986. In 1992 he completed his PhD on the Perceptual Aspects of Dutch Intonation under the supervision of Bob Ladd. Since then, he has taught phonetics at the universities of Edinburgh, Aarhus (Denmark), Hasselt (Belgium) and Antwerp (Belgium). He is now affiliated with City University London where he is a Reader in Phonetics in the Department of Language and Communication Science. Jo Verhoeven specializes in phonetics and motor speech disorders.

Preface

This volume is a collection of chapters on a topic which we felt deserved to be given a higher profile than it currently enjoys: the production and perception of prosodic features of speech amongst those who present with atypical speech and language profiles. We also wanted to present the implications of research focusing on this area for therapeutic practice. Research conducted in a vacuum is of little use to anyone; here, the authors attempt to show the impact of their work and the work of others on practice in speech and language therapy, and demonstrate the importance of continued research and development in this fascinating but oft-neglected area.

Prosody encompasses a number of different suprasegmental features of speech, including intonation – sometimes referred to as the music of speech – stress and accent placement, and speech rhythm. These features contribute to the listener's ability to correctly select items from the mental lexicon, to know when another speaker is finishing or preparing to speak further, to detect and indicate hierarchical relationships in conversations (e.g., peer–peer, teacher–student), to decide where emphasis has been placed in an utterance, and to understand another speaker's emotional state. Descriptions of intonation in English can be found in Halliday (1967), Cruttenden (1997), Roach (2009) and Wells (2006), among others, and see also Peppé (this volume). As a typical speaker of a language, one masters prosodic features and learns to use them appropriately to signal grammatical, discoursal and pragmatic meaning in the language; that is, the phonological function of prosodic features. In atypical speech, however, there may be an impairment or delay in how these functions are acquired from a developmental point of view or, alternatively, damage to the parts of the brain associated with speech or due to aging may result in atypical prosodic patterns later in life. In either scenario, this can affect the ability of the individual to produce and/or perceive prosodic cues, and can also have an effect on the interlocutor, resulting in a breakdown of communication or a misunderstanding of the intention of one or other of the participants. Clearly, then, this is an area of importance in research and remediation.

Sadly, however, prosodic features are often overlooked in assessment and remediation as they can be viewed as less tangible than individual segments (i.e., phonemes and allophones) and therefore rather challenging to address. This book, we hope, as well as providing a snapshot of recent research in this area, will go some way to helping speech and language therapists understand the importance of considering prosodic features when drawing up a programme of therapy, identify exactly what the issues are, help find ways to identify them, and provide ideas of how they can be remediated.

Part I of the book comprises four chapters which look at developmental disorders. In our first contribution, Sue Peppé outlines the aims of assessing prosodic abilities, and the importance of deciding whether atypical prosody is a primary or a secondary disorder and at what level the disorder occurs (sensory, motor, cognitive). She then goes on to consider how atypical prosody can affect interaction. After a review of assessment methods, Peppé details her own research into speech prosody amongst children with high-functioning autism; this includes a description and critique of the innovative computerized test battery Profiling Elements of Speech Communication (PEPS-C), which incorporates tests on the function and form of intonation in six different linguistic domains, and has been successfully applied to the assessment of speech prosody in a number of clinical studies (see, e.g., Stojanovik & Setter, this volume).

Following on from this, Stojanovik and Setter compare the results of two studies using the PEPS-C battery on groups of children with different genetic disorders: Williams syndrome and Down's syndrome. The chapter highlights the importance of studies in areas such as this in providing a window on the relationship between different genotypes and various cognitive domains; this window can allow us to hypothesize about the functions and development of language in typical language processing through the comparison of typical and atypical groups of speakers. The study shows that, although children with Williams and Down's syndromes have similar profiles in terms of receptive language level and non-verbal abilities when judged using standardized tests commonly applied in clinical situations, it should not be assumed that this entails a similarity in their performance on tasks such as those in the PEPS-C battery or, by extension, similarities in their receptive and expressive behaviour when in real communicative situations. The authors therefore call for further study on the pragmatic aspects of speech competence and performance in these two speaker groups.

The next two chapters use techniques from conversational analysis to look not only at the atypical speakers in their samples but also at the speech of the interlocutors, in order to establish whether there are observable patterns in interactional settings amongst the parties involved. Christina Samuelsson and colleagues investigate interactional speech prosody between Swedish children with language impairment and the non-impaired adults (speech and language therapists) involved in the interactions. Adopting an experimental framework which uses both acoustic and sequential analysis, the latter informed by conversational analysis techniques, the authors aim to show whether there is any system in speech and language therapists' use of prosody when using a certain test package as against interaction of an informal, personal nature, and whether the children respond to the patterns in a particular way. What is revealed is that the therapists do tend to use predictable, stereotypical prosodic patterns in their interactions with the children when using the test package, and also that their pitch range is less varied than when asking unscripted questions. More interestingly, the language-impaired children orient their prosodic features to that of the therapist, but do so in a way that indicates they can orient the prosodic form of an utterance but not necessarily the prosodic function; this may lead to communication issues at the discourse level. Samuelsson and colleagues conclude that prosody needs to be assessed in a variety of settings in order to have the most impact.

It is often claimed that children with a diagnosis of high-functioning autism have difficulty with social inclusion because of their atypical speech patterns, particularly in deficit-focused research. Taking a case-study approach, Deborah Kelly and Suzanne Beeke set out to examine the features of speech prosody and their interaction with the turn-taking ability of a 7-year-old child with high-functioning autism. Unlike Samuelsson and colleagues' study, Kelly and Beeke analyze video recordings of spontaneous speech between the child and his mother; the speech is then subjected to detailed sequential conversational analysis. Kelly and Beeke demonstrate that the child is most frequently able to use turn-taking cues successfully, but that on occasion there is a mismatch between the prosodic cues he uses and his intention to hold on to the turn. Whilst admitting that the findings of a single case study are impossible to generalize to the entire population of children with high-functioning autism, the authors call for inclusion of techniques derived from such studies as theirs to enable clinicians and caregivers to evaluate the communicative abilities of atypical speakers in context, and indicate how this might be achieved by giving an example of how the first author addressed the problem as a follow-up to the study.

Part II includes three chapters on speech prosody in acquired disorders, starting with a contribution from Jo Verhoeven and Peter Mariën, who look at suprasegmental aspects of Foreign Accent Syndrome in a 58-year-old female stroke patient. The subject's accent was reported by family and friends to have changed from her native (Belgian) Dutch to French; this impression was verified experimentally by 127 listeners who were native speakers of Dutch. The authors show how the prosodic features in the subject's speech remain largely undisturbed; however, speech rhythm is more consistent with that of a 'syllable-timed' language such as French, and this may be a contributing factor to the perceived foreignness of the accent. There is also evidence of a developing strategy to hold on to the speaker's turn in conversation, signalled by prosodic features.

As this book demonstrates, speakers with differing impairments can have unusual prosody. Whether these suprasegmental features have their origin in peripheral or central speech productive or perceptual processing, or in psycho-social difficulties, in all cases there is advantage in having access to accurate quantification. In our next chapter, Evelyn Abberton and Adrian Fourcin show how quantitative physical measurement with direct reference to vocal fold vibration can be matched to relevant aspects of speech production and perception, and provide visual patterns of pitch, loudness and phonation type in connected speech. These measurements and displays can supplement, and offer insights into, qualitative linguistic descriptions of prosody, including the elusive percept of 'tone of voice'. The authors show how the measures and real-time displays, directly related to production and perception, can be used for patterned biofeedback in therapy and teaching, and contribute to evidence-based practice. The analyses and displays shown in this chapter are produced using software running on a laptop, and both microphone signals and those captured from the larynx are used.

Our final contribution, from Gwen Van Nuffelen, addresses the issue of speech prosody in dysarthria, a motor-control disorder, offering suggestions on how to assess and remediate atypical patterns amongst dysarthria patients based on a variety of studies in this area. The author gives a comprehensive review of the literature, including information on how different types of dysarthria present with different disturbances to prosodic cues in speech, and how listeners might be able to find ways to cope with the speech of dysarthric speakers, before going on to recommend possible ways forward for the clinician. Suggestions include helping the client reduce speech rate which, together with an increased number of pauses or pause duration, can enable the dysarthric speaker to be more intelligible to a listener by giving the listener a greater amount of processing time. Techniques for achieving this are discussed, including pacing, hand- or finger-tapping, and the use of delayed auditory feedback devices.

This book had its beginnings in a one-day workshop, 'Speech Prosody in Atypical Populations', or SPiAP 2007, held in April 2007 at the University of Reading, UK. In addition to those whose contributions are written up for this collection, we would like to thank all the participants at the workshop for making it such a valuable and stimulating day. The workshop was partly supported by a grant from an anonymous donor (you know who you are), and also by the School of Psychology and Clinical Language Sciences at the University of Reading, to whom the editors express their gratitude. The book would not have been possible without the support of the publishers, J & R Press, and in particular the vision, enthusiasm and guidance of Rachael Wilkie, who has been a delight to work with and to whom we give our most heartfelt thanks.

Vesna Stojanovik

Jane Setter

February 2011

References

Cruttenden, A. (1997) *Intonation,* 2nd edition. Cambridge: Cambridge University Press.

Halliday, M.A.K. (1967) *Intonation and Grammar in British English.* The Hague: Mouton.

Peppé, S. (2011) Assessment of prosodic ability in atypical populations, with special reference to high-functioning autism. In V. Stojanovik & J. Setter (Eds) *Speech Prosody in Atypical Populations: Assessment and remediation.* Guildford: J&R Press Ltd, pp. 1–23.

Roach, P. (2009) *English Phonetics and Phonology,* 4th edition. Cambridge: Cambridge University Press.

Stojanovik, V. & Setter, J. (2011) Prosody in two genetic disorders: Williams and Down's syndrome. In V. Stojanovik & J. Setter (Eds) *Speech Prosody in Atypical Populations: Assessment and Remediation.* Guildford: J&R Press Ltd, pp. 25–43.

Wells, J.C. (2006). *English Intonation: An Introduction.* Cambridge: Cambridge University Press.

Part I

Developmental Disorders

Chapter 1

Assessment of prosodic ability in atypical populations, with special reference to high-functioning autism

Sue Peppé, Research Fellow, Queen Margaret University, Edinburgh

Introduction: What is prosody and why does it matter?

As explained in the Introduction, prosody encompasses intonation, rhythm and sentence stress – the suprasegmental aspects of speech. In this sense, intonation particularly deals with the pitch contours of speech, the realisation of the fundamental frequency of speech sounds, which are most noticeable at the endings of chunks of speech or of conversational turns. 'Intonation' is sometimes used as a superordinate term for the whole topic, but in this paper the term 'prosody' is preferred. Speech-rhythm derives from the timing frequency with which prominent syllables occur: seldom strictly rhythmical, but nevertheless a 'beat' is usually perceptible, at least in English. Sentence stress is concerned with information-structure; it shows where emphasis occurs, indicating the focus or main point of an utterance. This catalogue in itself reveals quite a range of topics, all included in the term 'prosody', and all having very different but important functions in speech. How is it, then, that prosody features so little in our consciousness? One clue is in that description of intonation: that pitch contours are most noticeable at phrase boundaries or conversational turn ends. We are particularly sensitive to them in this position because that is where they have most communicative effect; where a slight variation in contour can convey different attitudes (sarcasm, enthusiasm, reservation, protest, surprise) or signal various cues to turn-taking (I have finished, I have more to say, I need information from you, etc.). There may be just as much pitch-variation earlier in utterances, but because it has less communicative function we define it and notice it less. This means that the elements of prosody, such as pitch variation, sometimes have much function and sometimes little, are sometimes important and noticeable but sometimes not; and this in part explains the elusive, somewhat 'invisible' nature of prosody.

Prosody can be disordered in a number of clinical conditions; examples of these include Parkinson's disease, hearing loss, Williams Syndrome, specific language impairment (SLI), dyslexia and autism spectrum conditions. It can have a striking impact on intelligibility (to be explored in more detail below), as well as on a speaker's social capabilities. Prosodic impairment can operate at different neurological levels, from sensorimotor skills to cognitive processing. It can comprise not only expressive disorder, as when a person's speech sounds atypical, but also receptive disorder, in which a person's understanding or perception of prosody is impaired, although this is far less apparent. It interacts with other aspects of language as well as pragmatic and social skills, and the possible contribution of all these need to be taken into account. Several protocols have been devised to assess prosodic impairment; these will be considered below.

Aims of assessment

Goals

The aims of assessing prosodic abilities alter according to the primary interests of those designing the procedure: medicine, linguistic theory, language teaching and speech and language therapy to name but a few are all fields interested in prosody. A medical concern might be to characterize prosody as manifested in the various conditions in which it occurs, such as autism, dysarthria, Parkinson's Disease, foreign accent syndrome, hearing loss. Assessments to establish prosodic ability in such conditions are likely to focus on the perceived prosodic problems associated with the condition, and thus be limited in the aspects of prosody they cater for. In contrast, a linguistic theoretician might wish to establish a general picture of prosodic ability regardless of any condition that might affect it; perhaps to examine its relationship to language, or to discover prosodic developmental milestones. Assessments with this aim in view range more widely, considering the aspects of communication in which prosody has a role, receptive as well as expressive ability, and the interaction of prosody with linguistic factors such as grammar and segmental features, and with non-linguistic factors such as situational context and emotion.

Primary or secondary disorder?

For the clinician, a paramount concern must be to know whether a prosodic disorder is primary or secondary: whether it is directly a matter of prosody and the many factors which comprise it, or whether it arises from, say, an underlying sensory or motor problem or an interacting cognitive problem, in which case such problems need to be addressed first. As far as the clinician is concerned, the 'medical' approach to prosody assessment is likely to provide a picture of the immediate concrete problems to be handled; the second ('linguistic') approach would, however, be more likely to throw light on relevant secondary factors. For example, several studies sought to investigate prosody in autism by examining the prosodic 'symptoms', such as misplaced stress in speech (Baltaxe, Simmons & Zee, 1984; Baltaxe & Guthrie, 1987). A more holistic approach to the study of prosody in autism included the assessment of receptive as well as expressive ability and found receptive deficits (Peppé, McCann, Gibbon, O'Hare & Rutherford, 2007) which do not manifest as clearly as expressive ones. Clinically, it would be argued that receptive problems need to be addressed before an improvement in expressive ability can be expected. There is therefore likely to be more value, even for medical/clinical concerns, in adopting the holistic approach.

Level of processing

Apart from the mode (receptive or expressive), a thorough investigation of prosody should establish at what level a prosodic problem occurs. Underlying sensory problems may include hearing loss, which diminishes the ability to hear some fundamental frequencies but can also reduce ability to distinguish other kinds of prosodic variation. Differences of pitch-height, amplitude, on-syllable pitch-change and syllable-duration are considered to be the building-blocks of prosody, and will be referred to here as prosodic forms. Underlying motor problems may include insufficient control or inability to produce variation in these prosodic forms. There is no one-to-one equivalence between prosodic forms and the functions they convey, but forms cluster in differing combinations for specialized functional purposes: stress for example, involves variation in loudness, length and pitch (more of each for stressed syllables, but not necessarily involving all three parameters), while phrase- boundary is effected by combinations of lengthening, on-syllable pitch change and pausing; the exponents of prosodic stress and phrase-boundary can vary according to language and regional accent.

At a less basic level, there may be cognitive deficits, such as a lack of understanding of the functional differences that prosody can convey. It is also important to take into account the variations in communicative purpose that speakers may have: people with Williams syndrome tend to display prosody that sounds very enthusiastic, but recent research (Setter, Stojanovik, van Ewijk and Moreland, 2007) suggests that this is not the expression of genuine emotion. Similarly, at the other extreme, people with Parkinson's disease generally have depressed-sounding prosody: they may indeed be depressed, but their prosody is not so much an indication of their true feelings as a result of their motor inability to produce the pitch-range and pitch-level of the magnitude associated with unimpaired speakers (Schroder et al., 2009). People with autism tend to interpret the world literally and may have poor understanding of the implicit nature of prosody and the subtle effects it can convey.

Expressive prosody: Misleading, inappropriate or unusual?

There are more difficulties with assessing expressive prosody than with assessing other aspects of phonology such as articulation. Only a few aspects of prosody have the kind of fixed norms and roles in speech that, for example, consonants do. An example of a prosodic norm is the canonical lexical stress-pattern: in a word such as 'billow' the stress is always placed on the first syllable ('**bil**low'); in 'below', on the second ('be**low**').assuming stable pronunciation, i.e. [ɪ] in the first syllable in both cases, as opposed to schwa in 'below'. In this example, stress has the function of distinguishing meaning: if the stress-pattern is wrong, it indicates a different word, and the wrong stress-pattern can thus be misleading. In a word such as 'longhand' the stress should again be on the first syllable ('**long**hand'); if it is on the second ('long**hand**'), it makes the hearer think the stress has a different function: that of drawing attention to the second syllable, implying that the speaker wishes to emphasize it for some reason. Such a functional effect may be inappropriate. The possibility of changing the linguistic meaning or the pragmatic emphasis does not however apply in general to canonical stress-patterns: the word 'table' should have the stress on the first syllable ('**ta**ble'), and if the stress is on the second syllable ('ta**ble**'), the word sounds unusual. It will probably be still intelligible, because no other meaningful interpretation is available. Listeners try to infer meaning from what they hear, to the point of 'mis'-hearing segments (but not stress-patterns) in order to extract a meaningful result (Cutler, 1984). The misplaced stress in the case of 'table' is therefore likely to hinder processing but not cause misunderstanding; and might make the hearer wonder whether the speaker's English is non-native.

Such prosodic norms are rare, however, and for the most part prosodic 'errors' do not make the hearer think there is something wrong, but that the speaker has another agenda, often involving the conveying of emotion. As mentioned earlier, disordered prosody in people with Williams' syndrome can suggest non-existent enthusiasm; in Parkinson's disease, unwarranted depression. The task is to distinguish what is due to emotion or speaking intention, and what is attributable to poor prosody; and then to ascertain what aspect of prosody is giving rise to the misleading impression.

Interacting factors

Prosody does not exist in a vacuum; it is not the only conveyor of emotions or linguistic meaning. Voice quality and articulatory setting, facial expressions and body language, context, articulation, vocabulary and grammatical structures all contribute. One obvious consequence of this is that if prosody is disordered there are plenty of other factors to convey speaker intention, and it may be thought that prosody is therefore not all that important: that the message will be conveyed nonetheless. In communication disorders, however, speech is often truncated, with the result that there is less information from all factors. Then factors such as grammatical structures, which manifest themselves in relatively long stretches of speech, have a reduced role; prosody, by contrast, becomes more important. When utterances consist of a single word, intonation can indicate the type of utterance (question, statement, exclamation) and the speaker's attitude, and are thus important for interaction and social functioning.

To ascertain whether a speech problem is caused by prosodic deficit, it is important to be sure that assessment tasks address prosody and not a combination of prosody and other factors in which the other factors have a significant disambiguating role. For example, tasks to ascertain the ability to place lexical stress correctly sometimes ask the speaker to produce pairs of words which apparently vary only in their stress-pattern, but in many of the pairs (e.g. 'record' and 'record': Paul, Augustyn, Klin & Volkmar, 2005) the vowel quality of the first syllable is a significant distinguishing feature as well as the stress, and a simple lexical judgement will not indicate whether the hearer was judging the utterance by the segmental or the prosodic factor. On the other hand, the use of vowel quality that is not consistent with a stress-pattern (as in, for example, / `ricod /) can be either unintelligible or severely impede processing, and it is necessary to distinguish the elements, prosodic and segmental, that contribute to this. When both prosodic disorder and segmental distortion are present, lack of intelligibility is likely to increase considerably. A nice example of this is given in an exchange reported in Gilbert (2005) in which a person with non-native English asks for a 'resistor' in a shop, but places the stress on the first syllable. Although he tries several segmental variants of the word, he is misunderstood until he points to an example of what he wants. Of course, the segmental distortion is a contributory factor, and the misplaced stress does not account entirely for the misunderstanding, but it is possible to imagine that, with the stress in the right place, variations in the realisation of the segments would be barely noticeable.

Assessment methods

As previously stated, tests to evaluate prosodic ability have been devised. Nearly all of these are unstandardized, apart from the PVSP (see below).

Tennessee Test of Rhythm and Intonation Patterns (T-TRIP): Koike & Asp, 1981

This test is for general use in communication disorders, appropriate for both children and adults. One study that uses this protocol is an examination of prosody in children with Childhood Apraxia of Speech (CAS) by Peter and Stoel-Gammon (2008). The T_TRIP assesses production of prosody forms only, testing the speaker's ability to imitate various commonly-occurring speech-rhythms and intonation contours.

Prosody Profile (ProP): Crystal, 1982

Another test for general use, primarily designed for children but also appropriate for adults, the ProP also assesses only expressive prosody; it was used, for example, by Vance (1994) to establish prosodic disorder in a case study of a man with dysarthria. Instead of imitation, the ProP samples spontaneous speech. The prosody of the sample is transcribed with consideration mainly for intonation contours and functional prosodic categories (such as stress and phrase-boundary): occurrences of these are counted. It is thus more concerned with the functional effectiveness of prosody than the tests considered so far.

Prosody-Voice Screening Profile (PVSP): Shriberg, Kwiatkowski & Rasmussen, 1990

Like the ProP, the PVSP involves spontaneous speech sampling and transcription for counting major functional prosodic categories; it also includes consideration of vocal qualities. Like the other tests considered so far, it is appropriate for children and adults and concerned with expressive prosody only, not receptive ability. The PVSP, like the T-TRIP, has been used to investigate prosody in CAS (Odell & Shriberg, 2001); it has also been used to examine prosody in autism (Shriberg, Paul, McSweeny, Klin, Cohen & Volkmar, 2001; McSweeny & Shriberg, 2001).

Parts of assessments for other purposes

Protocols to assess prosodic skills are included as part of evaluations for conditions where communication can be affected. For example, dysarthria has a major deleterious effect on speech motor control, and therefore dysarthria assessments (Robertson, 1982; Enderby, 1983; Drummond, 1993) examine the ability of people with dysarthria to speak loudly and quietly; the extent of their pitch-range; their ability to imitate utterances with stress in the same place and how rapidly they can speak (diadochokinetic – DDK – assessment: the number of times in a minute a syllable can be repeated). Such assessments are largely concerned with prosodic forms rather than functions because forms are likely to be affected by a loss of speech motor control.

Similarly, hearing impairment is another condition in which prosody can be impaired. The PETAL (Phonological Evaluation and Transcription of Audio-visual Language: Parker, 1999) assessment includes some tasks to assess whether stress is produced correctly.

Protocols for research studies

Because of the lack of formalized prosody assessments, numerous procedures have been designed for assessing prosodic ability in prosody research projects. Some of these are designed to be used more widely as clinical tools; for example, the Swedish prosodic assessment procedure (Samuelsson, Scocco & Nettelbladt,

2003), which was designed specifically with children with SLI in mind. Many research protocols have informed later designs of prosody tasks; for example, such studies as the assessment of the ability to produce prosodic boundary (Katz, Beach, Jenouri and Verma, 1991) and the expression of attitude (Cruttenden, 1985).

Several studies have been conducted into the assessment of prosodic ability in people with autism spectrum disorders. These were reviewed in McCann and Peppé (2003); since then a comprehensive approach to the assessment of prosody in autism was devised for a project reported by Paul et al. (2005). This study tested (unusually) receptive as well as expressive skills and addressed stress, boundary and intonation, at both form and function levels.

The ability to place word stress correctly has been the subject of many studies, reviewed in Martínez-Castilla and Peppé (2010). It is noticeable that some areas of prosody come in for more assessment than others; stress is a favourite area, while boundary and the use of intonation to express attitude are less popular. It is possible that the reason for this is that the norms in the use of stress, such as canonical lexical stress patterns and the prescriptions of information structure (referred to earlier), make impairment more apparent than the other more fluid areas of prosody.

Assessment methodology: General strategies

Contrary to the earlier practices of collecting data by conducting imitation tasks or sampling and transcribing speech, the current vogue appears to be for eliciting prosody (or prosodic discrimination) through the use of minimal pairs. The main advantages of using minimal pairs are that this strategy obviates (a) the need for transcription and (b) the problem of deciding what the speaker's agenda is. Avoiding transcription is clearly an advantage, since systems for prosody transcription are unsettled. The following example is an illustration of the second problem. In a sample of a speaker's conversation, a word may appear to be wrongly stressed according to information-structure rules (new material is stressed, given material is de-accented); but the speaker may have a personal reason for stressing (or re-stressing) the word, and there is no way of ascertaining this. McCaleb and Prizant (1985) investigated the use of contrastive stress in four children with autism, with an example of wrongly placed stress in the following exchange:

Teacher: 'Yes, you found your own toothbrush.'
Johnny: 'TOOTHbrush. Johnny TOOTHbrush.'

Information structure would suggest that Johnny should not stress his second utterance of 'toothbrush', because he has mentioned it before and it is therefore 'given'; instead, the new material 'Johnny' should be stressed. However, Johnny might have a number of reasons for focusing on the word 'toothbrush' – e.g., clarifying the word, or emphasizing its pronunciation – which would make it correct, according to his agenda, to stress 'toothbrush'.

Approaches using strategies other than imitation, counting occurrences in a sample and minimal pair distinction have also been devised: one such approach uses conversation analysis, the advantages and disadvantages of which are described in Wells and Local, 2009, and Peppé, 2009b.

Acoustic analysis of prosody is increasingly available as technology develops. This makes it important to establish and clarify the combinations of prosodic forms that underlie prosodic exponency. Cues to prosodic functions can be traded with each other; for example, as suggested earlier, stress can be indicated by variation in any or all of the parameters pitch, duration and loudness, but a reduction in one will be compensated by an increase in another. Effective variation of this kind needs to be described and established, or there is a risk that this analysis will not be able to capture the realities of how prosody can be used. A reliable basis for acoustic analysis will, however, mean that the assessment of expressive prosody can be automated, and at least one laboratory is making good progress towards this (van Santen, 2009; Hosum, 2009).

Prosody in autistic spectrum conditions: Research project procedures

There follows a description of a particular research project, devised to investigate prosodic ability in school-age children with high-functioning autism (HFA). This project used a prosody test, PEPS-C (Peppé & McCann, 2003), that has recently been developed to provide a comprehensive assessment of prosodic skills, addressing the most widely-used functions of prosody in conversation; receptive and expressive abilities; and two levels of processing: the test will be described in some detail. This project has been described more fully in Peppé et al. (2007), but the methodology and results are described here to illustrate the potential of the test to quantify prosodic skills and deficits. Disordered prosody has been noted as a feature of ASC since it was first described (Kanner, 1942), but attempts to establish its nature had produced somewhat conflicting results (McCann and Peppé, 2003).

Participants

In this project, children with HFA and typically-developing controls were matched on a measure of receptive vocabulary acquisition (British Picture Vocabulary Scales, BPVS-II: Dunn, Dunn, Whetton & Burley, 1997), because we wished to control for language ability as distinct from prosodic ability. Since children in the HFA group had clinically significant preschool language delay, their receptive vocabulary lagged considerably behind those of typically-developing children of their own age. The TD group were therefore younger than the HFA group.

Participant groups were as follows:

- 31 children with HFA, 24 boys, 7 girls, age range 6;1 to 13;6 ($M = 9;10$, $SD = 2.3$);

- 72 children with typical development, 54 boys, 18 girls, age range 4;10 to 11;8 ($M = 6;10$, $SD = 1.5$).

We included the control group of typically-developing children because the test is not standardized. Inclusion criteria for the group with TD were that they should have a verbal mental age > 4;0 years; no significant hearing loss or visual impairment; no major physical disability or structural abnormality of the vocal tract; English as the first language and the language of the home; and that they had been resident in the Edinburgh area of Scotland for at least three years. The control group is much larger than the experimental group so that children could also be matched on socioeconomic status.

Criteria for inclusion in the group with HFA were similar with regard to hearing, physical disability, eyesight, and ambient language. They were also to be in the age range 6 to 13 years, with a verbal mental age > 4;0 years and reports of nonverbal ability within the normal range.

The diagnosis of autism, made by multidisciplinary assessment, was based on ICD 10 (World Health Organisation, 1993) or DSM-IV (pervasive developmental disorders: American Psychiatric Society, 1994), and a range of other autism assessment tools: the Childhood Autism Rating Scale (DiLalla and Rogers, 1994), Gilliam Autism Rating Scale (Gilliam, 1995), and Autism Diagnostic Observation Schedule (Lord, Risi, Lambrecht, Cook, Leventhal & DiLavore, 2000). Diagnosis also took account of clinical observations with regard to communication, reciprocal social interaction and repetitive behaviours, noting the children's ability to comprehend, imitate, use and attend to language; to interact socially; and to play appropriately with toys. Children previously diagnosed with Asperger syndrome were not selected; a subsequent study investigated the prosody of 40 children with Asperger's syndrome, and is the subject of a further research paper (Peppé, Cleland, O'Hare, Gibbon & Martínez-Castilla, 2011).

Prosody assessment: Profiling Elements of Prosody in Speech-Communication: PEPS-C

The PEPS-C test was designed in response to the lack of comprehensive prosody tests, and the problems posed by existing ones. It assesses several areas of prosody (pragmatic or interactional, affective, and grammatical or linguistic). Parallel tasks assess both receptive and expressive ability. Tasks are at two levels: that of form processing, requiring non-cognitive skills and that of communicative function, involving cognitive processes. The test adopts the minimal pair approach for functional distinctions; for prosodic forms it involves the production of prosodic variation through imitation and the assessment of discrimination ability via same-different tasks.

PEPS-C prosodic functions

PEPS-C samples prosodic functions grouped under four headings. One is interactional: Turn end tasks test the use of intonation to indicate what conversational response is appropriate, i.e., does the utterance 'apple' sound as though it is being offered (a question: 'apple?') or read from a book (a statement: 'apple.'). Another is affective: the Affect tasks assess the indication of liking or reservation by means of intonation and vocal quality, in this case with respect to certain foods. A third use is grammatical or linguistic: Chunking tasks assess the signalling of prosodic phrase boundaries, as in the grouping of colours in an utterance such 'red&pink and black socks' versus 'red and pink&black socks', or the grouping of foods in a phrase such as 'chocolate-biscuits and jam' versus 'chocolate, biscuits and jam'. A fourth use is pragmatic: in Focus tasks, emphasis (stress/accent) makes single words prominent to draw attention to them in order to contrast them with another word.

PEPS-C function task methodology

The test uses elicitation rather than conversation sampling, to avoid the problems of interpreting conversational agendas. Receptive task responses are elicited by the presentation of auditory stimuli to which the response is the choice of pictures (displayed on a computer screen) representing alternative meanings that the stimulus might convey. Expressive responses are elicited by the presentation of one picture on the screen and an invitation to produce the utterance suggested by the picture. Elicitation has the virtue that testees have to generate the words and the prosody simultaneously, as in normal conversation; but whereas conversational utterances vary widely in content, utterances elicited in this fashion are likely to vary little. The prosody of different testees can thus be compared in a way that is otherwise only available from imitation tasks where the utterances are effectively scripted.

Items used in the tasks and represented in the pictures are culturally inoffensive. The pictures included in the test are likely to be familiar to young children, and testees complete a pre-test vocabulary check to ensure that they can name the pictures. Segmentally, the items are easy to pronounce. The test is suitable for both adults and children, but children younger than the age of four do not on the whole have enough language competence to cope with it. The aim is to assess prosody that is ecologically valid, i.e., likely to be encountered in conversation. For this reason the reception task stimuli were agreed by at least two judges to indicate the meaning unambiguously but not exaggeratedly.

Stimuli are limited to minimal utterances so that prosody, as opposed to other linguistic variables, operates the disambiguation of meaning. For example, in the Focus tasks, grammatical structures (e.g., change of word-order) could indicate where emphasis is placed, but change of word-order is not available; in Chunking tasks, the introduction of additional conjunctions is similarly banned. The use of minimal utterances also increases the ecological validity of using prosody for disambiguation, since prosody becomes less essential where grammatical structures or lexis bear the main burden of conveying meaning. Short utterances also make it possible to assess the prosody skills of people with limited communication, who constitute those most likely to benefit from reliable use of prosody.

Scoring for the receptive tasks is done by the computer program. For the expressive tasks, responses are scored by a tester on a customized keypad out of sight of the screen: this avoids bias in the tester's judgement by knowledge of what the testee is looking at on the screen (item-order is randomized). In the Affect task, the correct response is the speaker's own preference; as the tester's only information on this is the intonation of the response, a verifying mechanism is introduced: after the testee has said the name of the food in a way that suggests liking or disliking, two faces (one displaying enthusiasm, the other dismay) appear, and the testee selects the one that matches his/her feelings about the food.

To avoid a heavy demand on auditory memory, only two response choices are offered for each item in reception tasks. Each task therefore comprises 16 items in order to have a reasonable number of non-chance scores (> 11 and < 5). A greater number would increase the non-chance scoring band, but the number of items was limited to 16 in order to keep the demands on attention as low as possible. Because of the relatively wide chance-band, children were deemed to have reached competence level in a task if their score was at least 12 (75%), rather than 50%. In expression tasks there was also a possibility of producing the right answer by chance, so the competence level was similarly set at 75%.

Responses to both receptive and expressive tasks are recorded on computer. This eliminates the possibility of errors in transference of data. Because of the binary nature of tasks, prosodic or intonational transcription skills are not needed. This also has the merit of avoiding the dubious areas of transcription methods.

PEPS-C form tasks

These were divided into Short-item tasks (one or two syllables) and Long-item tasks (six or seven syllables)[1].

Discrimination, for both Short- and Long-item tasks, follows a same–different format. Stimuli are from laryngograph signals taken from a microphone placed on the speaker's throat and recorded simultaneously with the function task stimuli. The sounds were taken from the laryngograph recording via a high-quality sound-card using 16-bit, 44100Hz, 705kps standard. In the Short-item Discrimination task, equal numbers of stimuli from the Affect and Turn end function tasks were used; for the Long-item Discrimination task, equal numbers of Chunking and Focus stimuli. The purpose of these tasks is to discover whether the testee's auditory processing is at a level that enables them to perceive the acoustic differences used in the function reception tasks. With hearing operating in free field (i.e., without headphones and using both ears), the testee hears a stimulus consisting of two sounds while two symbols, one representing 'Same'

---

1 These tasks are designated Intonation and Prosody respectively in the beta-version of PEPS-C currently in use by some researchers.

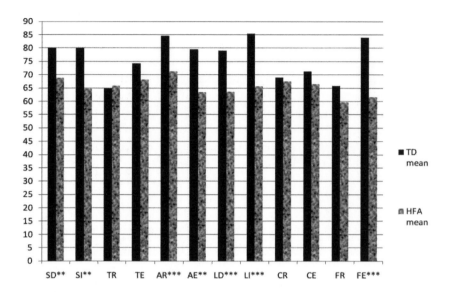

** : between-group difference on this task significant at <.01 level
*** : between-group difference on this task significant at <.001 level

Figure 1.1 Mean percentage prosody scores for HFA group and language-matched TD group

or one representing 'Different', appear on the computer screen. Using a mouse, the testee clicks on the symbol to go with the stimulus.

Expression form tasks (imitation) seek to elicit a prosodic repertoire by requiring testees to imitate words and phrases similar to those used in the reception function tasks, but with some additional aspects (e.g., more tones, more varied stress-placement). The instruction is to listen to the stimulus and repeat what they hear, copying exactly the way it is said. Responses are scored as Good (1 point) for a perfect imitation: intonation copied, prosodic function correctly represented, similar loudness and speech-rate; Fair (a half-point) where something is lacking, e.g. prosodic function ambiguous, intonation not precisely the same, loudness/speech-rate differing from the stimulus; and Poor (zero) where several or all aspects are mismatched. The test is accompanied by a training programme in which examples of good, fair and poor imitation are given and scored, to standardize judgements by testers. Errors can be noted from these tasks: these might include inability to imitate a particular type of intonation; tendencies to repeat the same intonation pattern; or overall habits of speech that differ from the stimuli on rhythm, volume, speech-rate or pitch-range.

Results

Statistical analyses, including standard deviations and score-ranges, are compared in Table 1.1. Mean percentage prosody scores by the two groups are shown in Figure 1.1.

It is worth remembering that the children were matched on a language measure. When matched on chronological age, the between-group differences were greater: highly significant in all tasks except one. While the language-matched comparison is interesting from the point of view of the relative contributions of prosody and language, the age-matched comparison is likely to be more relevant socially.

It will be observed that while the mean scores of children in the HFA group do not reach competence level (75%) on any task, this is also true of the TD group on some tasks. An earlier publication using the PEPS-C test (Wells, Peppé & Goulandris, 2004) suggests the ages at which typically-developing children acquire the prosody skills tested in PEPS-C. In line with earlier studies (e.g., Cruttenden 1985; Lloyd, Mann & Peers, 1998; Crystal, 1986; Beach, Katz & Skowronski, 1996), our findings indicate that prosody skills continue to develop during the school years.

Discussion: Advantages and disadvantages of the PEPS-C test

All children, in both the TD and HFA groups, were able to cooperate with and complete the tasks, including typically-developing children aged 4, except that one child with HFA failed to complete any expressive tasks. The time taken varied between forty minutes and an hour: apparently acceptable to the children involved and a reasonable variation considering the wide age range of participants. This is, however, a relatively long duration for the clinical assessment of one aspect of language.

The tasks where between-group differences were greatest were those where prosodic difficulties in the HFA group were expected to transpire, i.e., the understanding and expression of affect; the placement of contrastive stress;

Table 1.1 Statistical analysis of prosody scores

PEPS-C tasks	F (partial $\eta2$)	HFA group (N = 31)[a]		TD group (N = 72)[b]	
	df 1,97	SD	range	SD	range
Short-item Discrimination (SD)	7.01** (.07)	22	25.0–100	17.4	31.3–100
Short-item Imitation (SI)	10.94** (.10)	20.6	9.4–93.8	18	34.4–100
Turn-end Reception (TR)	.01 (.00)	21.4	18.7–100	18.1	31.3–100
Turn-end Expression (TE)	1.76 (.02)	21.8	43.7–100	18.1	31.3–100
Affect Reception (AR)	16.21*** (.14)	21.6	31.3–100	11.4	50.0–100
Affect Expression (AE)	11.32** (.10)	26.3	18.7–100	19.2	31.3–100
Long-item Discrimination (LD)	15.1*** (.13)	23.1	31.3–100	13.3	43.8–100
Long-item Imitation (LI)	36.83*** (.27)	22	34.4–100	11.4	37.5–100
Chunking Reception (CR)	.04 (.00)	15.7	43.7–93.8	15.6	37.5–93.8
Chunking Expression (CE)	1.35 (.01)	26.4	18.7–100	11.8	37.5–100
Focus Reception (FR)	2.53 (.02)	19	31.3–100	19.1	37.5–100
Focus Expression (FE)	45.8*** (.32)	26.4	18.7–100	15	56.3–100

discrimination between prosodic forms, and imitation tasks. The test can therefore be said to be successful to the extent that it reflects and quantifies results that were expected for this population. Inter-rater reliability on the test is acceptable (Wells et al., 2004; Peppé et al., 2007).

Quantification in this way, using mean scores from groups, hides what was apparent to the researchers: that there was great variability in the HFA group. This, however, would not be a disadvantage in assessing individuals in a clinical situation.

Researchers have used PEPS-C to assess prosody in other atypical populations; for example, in Williams syndrome (Stojanovik, Setter & van Ewijk, 2007) and in SLI and dyslexia (Marshall, Harcourt-Brown, Ramus & van der Lely, 2009). Projects using PEPS-C are ongoing in the assessment of prosody in people with hearing loss, with cochlear implants and with head injury. This suggests that the test is appropriate for various kinds of disorders.

There are two major disadvantages to PEPS-C. One is that it provides for no sampling or assessment of spontaneous conversation. There is thus no mechanism for checking whether the prosody and intonation used in the test by the testees, or their judgements about the functions of prosody, are carried over into their normal speech and conversation. The elicitation of the same prosodic function 16 times in succession bears little resemblance to the prosodic demands of conversation. Although little in the way of practice effects were found in PEPS-C scores (Wells and Peppé, 2003), it is likely, even appropriate, that prosodic exponency would modify in the course of completing a task. It is, however, possible to review conversation recorded between the testee and the tester during assessment. An example of how one child with HFA produced a conversational interaction reflecting his poor score on a PEPS-C task is described in Peppé, McCann, Gibbon, O'Hare and Rutherford, (2006). PEPS-C does not, however, capture or quantify the extent to which a person's prosody is perceived simply as atypical, without reference to its functionality. Results from an experiment in the perception of atypicality in the speech of children with and without ASC, relating atypical prosody to functional prosodic ability, are briefly reported in Peppé, Martínez-Castilla, Lickley, Mennen, McCann, O'Hare and Rutherford (2006).

The second disadvantage is that PEPS-C does not assess fine differences of processing levels: a division into 'form' and 'function' is crude. Nor does it give indications of the prosodic exponency of errors, i.e., whether a response is misleading because of the lack of a pause or because of an increase in pitch on the wrong syllable, for example. Recordings of responses can be subjected to acoustic analysis, but this requires further training. Automated assessment, when satisfactorily based on realistic prosodic exponency of functions, may provide a solution.

It must also be remembered that PEPS-C samples only a small cross-section of prosodic ability; it tests one way in which prosody can segment speech into grammatical units, one example of the expression of attitude, one function in which accent placement is important, and one dichotomy in conversational turn-endings. It provides no information about aspects of prosody that do not affect communication function in a concrete way, but may have an impact on social functioning or listenability; this is true of the more global aspects of prosodic form, such as speech-rhythm, pitch-range, loudness and speech-rate.

Other advantages of PEPS-C are that it potentially provides a benchmark for prosodic ability, that it assesses a fairly comprehensive set of prosodic skills, and that it is possible to compare receptive with expressive ability and form with function skills. The need to produce only short utterances is an advantage for clinicians working with clients with limited language, as is the lack of need for transcription skills. It can thus be said, perhaps, to be more usable than previous instruments.

Further developments

Because of the problems posed by the large number of items in a task, resulting in a wide band of chance scoring, potential fatigue, and (arguably) an unnecessarily long test, steps have been taken to develop a version of the test that offers more than two options for responses in the receptive tasks, and more than two scoring options for expressive tasks. This would mean that a meaningful result could be obtained with a smaller number of task items. In the prototype model, four, five and six options are available. Originally, options were limited to two in order to avoid too heavy a demand on auditory memory, but subsequently it has appeared that a neurotypical adult or child can discriminate prosodic differences with more than two response options. It remains to be seen to what extent prosodic stimuli can be held in mind while an increased number of options are reviewed. Accurate reaction times will also be provided; these will take into account the varying places in a response where it is valid to measure reaction times from. Both these features would allow for finer discrimination of prosodic ability.

Clearly standardization would be an improvement. At the moment, researchers need to collect their own normative data, and there is very little to provide a yardstick for clinicians. There is also the possibility of clinical intervention based on the approach adopted by the test.

A further area for development is to design tasks that would investigate prosody skills in children younger than four years old. This would be an advantage for investigating prosody problems at an earlier stage of language development, and provide necessary research in a current lacuna concerning the role of prosody in language acquisition. There have also been requests to include tasks that address lexical accent placement, to address the kinds of problems apparent in the 'resistor' example cited earlier: these are currently under development.

The PEPS-C test has been translated into French, Spanish, Dutch and Norwegian, as described in Peppé, Martínez-Castilla, Coene, Hesling, Moen, and Gibbon (2010). It is also available in various accents of English: UK General, UK Scottish, North American General and Australian General. Requests for translated versions have been received from researchers working in Finnish, Portuguese, Farsi, Chinese and Egyptian Arabic, and translation into more languages is a clear possibility. The test has also been used with learners of English (Setter, Stojanovik & Martínez-Castilla, 2010): this study provides evidence that prosody can be impaired in the learner's target language, and it is possible that language-learning could benefit from an approach based on the function-form distinctions exploited by the PEPS-C and parallel reception-expression prosody tasks. All this would help to increase awareness of prosody, remove its invisibility and lift it out of its present state as the 'Cinderella' of language skills.

References

American Psychiatric Society (1994) *Diagnostic and Statistical Mmanual for Mental Disorders*, 4th edn. Washington, D.C: American Psychiatric Publishing, Inc.

Baltaxe, C.A.M. & Guthrie, D. (1987) The use of primary sentence stress by normal, aphasic and autistic children. *Journal of Autism and Developmental Disorders, 17(2)*, 255–271.

Baltaxe, C.A.M., Simmons, J.Q. & Zee, E. (1984) Intonation patterns in normal, autistic and aphasic children. In A. Cohen & M. van de Broecke (Eds) *Proceedings of the 10th International Congress of Phonetic Sciences* (pp. 713–718). Dordrecht: Foris Publications.

Beach, C. M., Katz, W. F. & Skowronski, A. (1996) Children's processing of prosodic cues for phrasal interpretation. *Journal of Acoustical Society of America, 99(2)*, 1148–1160.

Cruttenden, A. (1985) Intonation comprehension in ten-year-olds. *Journal of Child Language, 12*, 643–661.

Crystal, D. (1986) Prosodic development. In P. Fletcher & M. Garman (Eds) *Language Acquisition: Studies in First Language Development*, 3rd edn. Cambridge: Cambridge University Press.

Crystal, D. (1982) *Profiling Linguistic Disability*. London: Arnold.

Cutler, E.A. (1984). Stress and accent in language production and understanding. In D. Gibbon & H. Richter (Eds) *Intonation, Accent and Rhythm: Studies in discourse phonology*. Berlin: Walter de Gruyter.

DiLalla, D.L. and Rogers, S.J. (1994). Domains of the Childhood Autism Rating Scale: Relevance for diagnosis and treatment. *Journal of Autism and Developmental Disorders, 24*, 115–128.

Dunn, L., Dunn, L., Whetton, C. & Burley, J. (1997) *The British Picture Vocabulary Scale*. Windsor: NFER-Nelson.

Drummond, S.S. (1993) *Dysarthria Examination Battery*. Tucson, Az: Communication Skill Builders.

Enderby, P. (1983) *Frenchay Dysarthria Assessment*. Austin, Tx: Pro-Ed.

Gilbert, J.B. (2005) *Clear Speech: Teacher's book: Pronunciation and Listening Comprehension in American English*, 3rd edn. Cambridge: Cambridge University Press.

Gilliam, J.E. (1995) *Gilliam Autism Rating Scale (GARS)*. Austin, Tx: PRO-ED.

Hosum, J. (2009) Computer processing for analysis of speech disorders. In R. Paul and P. Flipsen (Eds), *Child Speech Sound Disorders*. San Diego, CA: Plural Publishing.

Kanner, L. (1943). Autistic disturbances of affective contact. *Nervous Child, 2*, 217–250.

Katz, W.F., Beach, C.M., Jenouri, K. & Verma, S. (1996) Duration and fundamental frequency correlates of phrase boundaries in productions by children and adults. *Journal of Acoustical Society of America, 99(5)*, 3179–3191.

Koike, K.J.M. & Asp, C.W. (1981) Tennessee Test of Rhythm and Intonation Patterns. *Journal of Speech and Hearing Disorders, 46,* 81–87.

Lloyd, P., Mann, S. & Peers, I. (1998) The growth of speaker and listener skills from five to eleven years. *First Language, 18,* 81–103.

Marshall, C., Harcourt-Brown, S., Ramus, F. & van der Lely, H. (2009) The link between prosody and language skills in children with specific language impairment (SLI) and/or dyslexia. *International Journal of Language and Communication Disorders, 44,* 466–488.

Martínez-Castilla, P. & Peppé, S. (2010) Cross-linguistic expression of contrastive accent: Clinical assessment in Spanish and English. *Clinical Linguistics and Phonetics, 24(11),* 955–962.

McCaleb, P. & Prizant (1985) Encoding of new versus old information by autistic children. *Journal of Speech and Hearing Disorders, 50,* 226–230.

McCann, J. & Peppé, S. (2003) Prosody in autistic spectrum disorders: A critical review. *International Journal of Language and Communication Disorders, 38,* 325–350.

McSweeny, J.L. & Shriberg L.D. (2001) Clinical research with the prosody-voice screening profile. *Clinical Linguistics and Phonetics, 15 (7),* 505–528.

Odell, K.H. & Shriberg, L.D. (2001) Prosody-voice characteristics of children and adults with apraxia of speech. *Clinical Linguistics and Phonetics, 15 (4),* 275–307.

Parker, A. (1999) *PETAL: Phonological Evaluation and Transcription of Audio-visual Language.* Bicester, UK: Winslow.

Paul, R., Augustyn, A., Klin, A. & Volkmar, F. (2005) Perception and production of prosody by speakers with autistic spectrum disorders. *Journal of Autism and Developmental Disorders, 35,* 205–220.

Peppé, S.J.E. (2009) Aspects of identifying prosodic impairment: Scientific forum on prosody in speech-language pathology. *International Journal of Speech-Language Pathology, 11(4),* 332–338.

Peppé, S., Cleland, J., Gibbon, F., O'Hare, A. & Martínez-Castilla, P. (2011) Expressive prosody in children with autism spectrum conditions. *Journal of Neurolinguistics, 24,* 41–53.

Peppé, S., Martínez-Castilla, P., Lickley, R., Mennen, I., McCann, J., O'Hare, A. & Rutherford, M. (2006) Functionality and perceived atypicality of expressive prosody in children with autism spectrum disorders. In R. Hoffmann & H. Mixdorff (Eds), *Proceedings of the 3rd International Conference on Speech Prosody* (p. 93). Dresden: TUD Press.

Peppé, S.J.E., Martínez-Castilla, P., Coene, M., Hesling, I., Moen, I. & Gibbon, F. (2010) Assessing prosodic disorder in five European languages. *International Journal of Speech-Language Pathology, 12(1)*, 1-7.

Peppé, S., McCann, J., Gibbon, F., O'Hare, A. & Rutherford, M. (2006) Assessing prosodic and pragmatic ability in children with high-functioning autism. *Journal of Pragmatics, 38*, 1776-1791.

Peppé, S., McCann, J., Gibbon, F., O'Hare, A. & Rutherford, M. (2007) Receptive and expressive prosodic ability in children with high-functioning autism. *Journal of Speech Language and Hearing Research, 50*, 1015-1028.

Peter, B. & Stoel-Gammon, C. (2008) Central timing deficits in subtypes of primary speech disorders. *Clinical Linguistics and Phonetics, 22(3)*, 171-198.

Robertson, (1982) *Dysarthria Profile*. Tucson, Az: Communication Skill Builders.

Samuelsson, C., Scocco, C. & Nettelbladt, U. (2003) Towards assessment of prosodic abilities in Swedish children with language impairment. *Logopedics, Phoniatrics, Vocology, 28*, 156-166.

Schröder, C., Dengler, R. & Nikolova, Z.T. (2009) Changes of emotional prosody in Parkinson's disease. *Journal of Neurological Science*, downloaded 25.11.09.

Setter, J., Stojanovik, V. & Martínez-Castilla, P. (2010) Evaluating the intonation of non-native speakers using a computerised test battery. *International Journal of Applied Linguistics, 20(3)*, 368-385.

Setter, J., Stojanovik, V., van Ewijk, L. & Moreland, M. (2007) Affective prosody in children with Williams syndrome. *Clinical Linguistics and Phonetics, 9*, 659-672.

Stojanovik, V., Setter, J. & van Ewijk, L. (2007) Intonation abilities of children with Williams syndrome: A preliminary investigation. *Journal of Speech, Language, and Hearing Research, 50*, 1606-1617.

Shriberg, L., Kwiatkowski, J. & Rasmussen, C. (1990) *Prosody-Voice Screening Profile*. Tucson: Communication Skill Builders.

Shriberg, L.D., Paul, R., McSweeny, J.L., Klin, A., Cohen, D.J. & Volkmar, F.R. (2001). Speech and prosody characteristics of adolescents and adults with high-functioning autism and Asperger's Syndrome. *Journal of Speech, Language, and Hearing Research, 44,* 1097–1115.

Vance, J. (1994). Prosodic deviation in dysarthria: A case study. *European Journal of Communication Disorders, 29,* 61–76.

van Santen, J., Prud'hommeaux, E. & Black, L. (2009) Automated measures for assessment of expressive prosody. *Speech Communication, 51(11),* 1082–1097.

Wells, B., Peppé, S. & Goulandris, A. (2004) Intonation development from five to thirteen. *Journal of Child Language, 31,* 749–778.

Wells, B. & Peppé, S. (2003) Intonation abilities of children with speech and language impairment. *Journal of Speech, Language and Hearing Research, 46(1),* 5–20.

Wells, B. & Local, J. (2009) Prosody as an interactional resource: A clinical linguistic perspective. *International Journal of Speech-Language Pathology, 11(4),* 321–325.

World Health Organization (1993). *The ICD-10 Classification of Mental and Behavioural Disorders.* Geneva: World Health Organization.

Chapter 2

Prosody in two genetic disorders: Williams and Down's syndrome

Vesna Stojanovik, School of Psychology and Clinical Language Sciences, University of Reading, UK

Jane Setter, Department of English Language and Literature, University of Reading, UK

Introduction

The study of disorders of prosody in atypical populations has relatively recently become the focus of intense clinical linguistic research. In particular, interest has been centering on the study of prosody in populations affected by genetic disorders which are characterized by uneven cognitive profiles such that there are obvious strengths and weaknesses in different cognitive domains. Studying populations with clearly identifiable genotypes provides a unique opportunity to investigate the relationship between specific genotypes and different cognitive domains. In addition, populations affected with genetic disorders, in which the relationship between language and other cognitive functions might differ from what is seen in typical development, provide a natural experiment to determine how different cognitive aspects may be related to each other. The present chapter is concerned with the relationship between prosodic abilities on the one hand and receptive language and non-verbal skills on the other in two distinct atypical populations: children with Williams syndrome and those with Down's syndrome.

Williams syndrome (WS) is a relatively rare genetic disorder with a prevalence of 1 in 25,000 live births (Korenberg, Chen, Hirota, et al., 2000; Frangistakis, Ewart, Moris, et al., 1996), although a more recent study conducted in Norway reported an incidence rate of 1 in 7500 (Strømme, Bjømstad & Ramstad, 2002). WS results from a microdeletion on one of the long arms of chromosome 7, affecting the alleles of the elastin gene. This deletion results in a number of physical abnormalities, such as elevated blood calcium levels, sensitive hearing and high blood pressure, failure to thrive in infancy, abnormal sensitivity to certain classes of sounds (hypersacusis), and mild to moderate learning difficulties with IQ of between 40 and 60, on average (Udwin &Yule, 1991).

Down's syndrome (DS) is a very common genetic disorder which occurs approximately in 1 in 800 live births ("Down syndrome": http://www.nhs.uk/conditions/downs-syndrome/Pages/Introduction.aspx). It results from a genetic error in that the embryo receives three chromosomes 21, hence the often used term for DS is trisomy 21. The majority of cases with DS (about 97%) occur due to this type of genetic error. DS leads to a number of physical and cognitive abnormalities, such as short stature, hypothyroidism, hypotonia, congenital heart disease and mild to moderate learning difficulties with an average IQ range of between 40 and 60 (Prasher & Cunningham, 2001).

Both groups present with uneven but qualitatively different profiles of cognitive abilities despite similar levels of non-verbal IQ. Individuals with DS typically present with relatively good visuo-spatial abilities and poor expressive language skills (Jarrold, Baddeley & Hewes., 1999; Klein & Mervis, 1999; Chapman, Schwartz, & Kay-Raining Bird, 1991; Fowler, Gelman & Gleitman,1994; Fowler, 1990; Rondal & Comblain; 1996). Research also shows that speech and language are relatively more affected in individuals with DS compared to other populations with learning difficulties (Dodd & Thompson, 2001; Fowler, Gelman & Gleitman, 1994; Rondal 1993). In contrast, individuals with WS display relatively good expressive language abilities and poor visuo-spatial abilities (Bellugi, Marks, Bihrle & Sabo, 1988). Furthermore, both disorders present with characteristic language profiles specific to each disorder. Thus in late childhood and adulthood, morpho-syntactic abilities, vocabulary skills and expressive prosodic skills are relative weaknesses in DS (Stojanovik, in press; Pettinato & Verhoeven, 2009). In contrast, these abilities are on a par with general language and non-verbal abilities in WS (Stojanovik, Setter & van Ewijk, 2007).

Prosody in Williams and in Down's syndrome

The first published study of prosody in WS was by Reilly, Klima and Bellugi (1990), who investigated the use of affective prosody (pitch changes, vocalic lengthening and modifications in volume) in a story-telling task in a small group of adolescents with WS and those with DS. The study reported that adolescents with WS used significantly more affective expressive prosody compared to the adolescents with DS who were matched on mental age to the WS individuals, and compared to two groups of typically developing children (a group of 3- and 4-year-olds and a group of 7- and 8-year-olds). The authors concluded that the use of affective expressive prosody by adolescents with WS was abnormal, as they used the same levels of expressive prosody regardless of how many times they told the same story, and irrespective of the audience. This was not the case with the individuals with DS and with the typically developing children. Since this initial study into affective expressive prosody in WS, research into prosody in WS was somewhat dormant until recently with the publication of a pilot study by Catterall, Howard, Stojanovik, Szczerbinski and Wells (2006). This was the first study to investigate several aspects of both expressive and receptive prosodic skills, using specific experimental tasks from the manual version of the Profiling Elements of Prosody for Speech and Communication (PEPS-C) battery[2] (Wells & Peppé, 2001). The expressive and receptive prosodic skills of two adolescents with WS were compared to those of two control groups: a group matched for chronological age (CA), and a group matched for language abilities (LA). The study reported impaired expressive and receptive prosodic abilities in both adolescents with WS when compared to CA controls although not when compared to LA controls. A larger study by Stojanovik, Setter and van Ewijk (2007) included 14 children and teenagers with WS who were assessed on the computerized version of the PEPS-C battery by Peppé, McCann and Gibbon (2003) described in Chapter 1 (this volume), and this reported similar results to the Caterall et al. study. The children with WS did not differ from children matched for receptive language abilities on any of the expressive and receptive prosody tasks, apart from one task which assessed prosody form, i.e., the children's ability to repeat different intonation patterns over longer prosodic domains. However, the children with WS had significant prosodic deficits in a number of prosodic domains when compared to children of a similar chronological age, including the use of prosody to signal the most important word in an utterance (focus function), use of prosody to mark boundaries between words or phrases (chunking) and use of prosody for regulating conversational behaviour (turn-end). The only task on which the WS group did not differ from the CA controls was one that assessed the production and understanding of affect. Interestingly, however, a subsequent study involving the same participants (Setter, Stojanovik, van Ewijk & Moreland,

2 The battery was originally called Profiling Elements of Prosodic Systems – Child Version

2007) revealed that, despite there being no difference between the WS group and the two control groups regarding the production and comprehension of affect on the specific PEPS-C task, the WS group differed significantly from the typically developing controls in the level of pitch range displayed in a spontaneous speech task. Notably, their pitch range was much wider than that of the two control groups. This wide pitch range also contributed to the WS group being perceived by phonetically naïve listeners as sounding much more emotionally involved when telling a story than typically developing children of a similar chronological age and those of a similar language comprehension level (Setter et al., 2007).

Using a developmental trajectory approach, which allows one to investigate the possible causal mechanisms of how different cognitive skills may develop over time in terms of onset and rate of development compared to TD children (Thomas et al., 2009), Stojanovik (2010) found a number of important issues regarding linguistic prosody in WS. Firstly, there is a delayed onset in the development of the ability of children with WS to produce the focus function of prosody. Secondly, there is a delayed rate of development for the ability of children with WS to understand the focus function of prosody, and to produce and understand the chunking and turn-end functions of prosody. Such results are not surprising and they complement the findings by Nazzi, Paterson and Karmiloff-Smith (2003) who reported that infants with WS between 15 and 48 months show atypical sensitivity to stress patterns.

More recently, prosody has become the focus of investigation in individuals with WS speaking languages other than English. For example, Martínez-Castilla, Sotillo and Campos (2010) reported that Spanish speaking adolescents and adults with WS had prosodic deficits with the understanding and production of prosody on a Spanish adaptation of the PEPS-C battery (Martínez-Castilla & Peppé, 2008). In particular, the Spanish individuals with WS had difficulty with nonfinal contrastive focus. Indeed, when English and Spanish speaking individuals with WS were compared in a study by Martinez-Castilla, Stojanovik, Setter and Sotillo (in press), two main findings regarding prosodic function were found. Firstly, the English speaking children with WS performed significantly lower than the Spanish children with WS on the understanding of the affective function of prosody. This finding replicates an already reported difference in the study of typically developing English and Spanish speaking children (Martínez-Castilla & Peppé, 2008). Secondly, the Spanish speaking children with WS were much poorer than their English counterparts on the production of pre-final narrow focus, which was also shown to be the case in typically developing

Spanish and English speaking children in Martínez-Castilla and Peppé (2008). With regard to the issue of wider pitch range in individuals with WS, a study of French speaking children with WS by Lacroix, Stojanovik, Dardier and Laval (2010) also found wider pitch range in French speaking individuals with WS compared to chronological age-matched controls.

Compared to research into prosody in WS, which particularly recently has attracted wide interest, there is hardly any research in prosody in DS. An early study by Reilly et al. (1990), mentioned above, reported that adolescents with DS made less use of affective expressive prosody in a story telling task compared to adolescents with WS and were more in line with mental age matched typically developing children. Perception of prosody was not investigated in this study. Pettinato and Verhoeven (2009) investigated the processing of word stress in children and adolescents with DS and reported disrupted stress structure both at the levels of production and perception. Stojanovik (in press) reported that children with DS were particularly impaired on expressive aspects of prosody relative to language and non-verbal ability. Their receptive prosodic abilities were found to be as expected for their non-verbal abilities.

By investigating atypical populations with distinct and well-defined genotypes, such as individuals with WS and those with DS, we have the opportunity to find out more about the underlying architecture of cognitive organization. In particular, by comparing the linguistic abilities of two distinct genetic syndromes (inter-syndrome comparisons), we can identify syndrome specific profiles and gain more insight into the link between specific genotypes and resulting phenotypes.

The present chapter will focus on addressing the following issues:

1. How do the receptive and expressive prosodic abilities of children with WS compare to those of children with DS?

2. Are there syndrome-specific prosody profiles linked to the two different genotypes?

Methodology

Participants

There were four groups of participants: The first one was a group of nine children with WS aged between 6 and 13;11 (mean age = 9;3) recruited through the

Williams Syndrome Foundation in the UK. All children had a positive FISH (fluorescent in situ hybridization) test confirming a diagnosis of WS. The second group consisted of nine children with DS aged between 8;2 and 12;11 (mean age = 9;3) recruited through DownsEd International in the UK. They all had a trisomy 21, the most common cause of DS. There were two control groups. There was a group of younger typically developing (TD) children matched on non-verbal mental age to the WS and DS group aged between 4 and 7;7 (mean age = 5;3). The younger TD group was matched to the WS and DS groups on the basis of the scores from the Coloured Progressive Matrices. The fourth group were eight TD children matched on chronological age to the WS and DS groups and aged between 8;1 and 10;11 (mean age 9;8). The TD groups were recruited through schools in Reading and West Berkshire.

Materials

Prosody was assessed using a battery of tasks specifically designed to assess expressive and receptive prosody, Profiling Elements of Prosody for Speech

Table 1 Participants' raw scores on standardized tests

Group	TROG raw	RCM raw
DS (n=9)	5 (sd=1)	15 (sd=3)
WS (n=9)	8 (sd=3)	15 (sd=4)
TD (LA) (n=8)	6 (sd=2)	16 (sd=4)
TD (CA) (n=8)	19 (sd=1)	33 (sd=4)

and Communication (PEPS-C) (Peppé, McCann & Gibbon, 2003). The battery is already described in Chapter 1 (this volume) and therefore only a brief description of the tasks is included in the Appendix. All the participants were given a standardized language test, the Test for the Reception of Grammar (Bishop, 2003) in order to assess language comprehension, and a standardized non-verbal test, the Coloured Progressive Matrices (Raven, 2003) which assesses non-verbal cognitive abilities. Table 1 shows the scores on the standardized tests for the groups.

Procedure

The procedure was the same as that described in Stojanovik et al. (2007). The participants were tested individually either in a quiet room at their school, in their homes or in a dedicated laboratory at the University of Reading. The session lasted approximately 60–90 minutes. Prior to administering the PEPS-C battery, each child was administered a picture naming task. This vocabulary check was needed in order to ensure that the children were familiar with the lexical items which were later to appear in the prosody tasks. The tasks were presented in a random order to different participants to ensure that there were no presentation order effects. All the output tasks were recorded directly onto a laptop as well as on a DAT recorder as a backup. The output tasks were recorded with the PEPS-C software by using a Sony lapel microphone connected to a laptop (Toshiba, Intel Pentium Core Duo CPUT7250@2.00GHz 778MHz, Realtech High Definition Audio sound card). As established in the PEPS-C software, the tasks were recorded at a sampling frequency of 22.05 kHz.

Inter-rater reliability

The responses from 25 out of a total of 34 participants on the output tasks, having initially been rated by the researchers collecting the data, were independently rated by one of two trained phoneticians. Inter-rater agreement was calculated using kappa coefficient in order to account for chance agreement. Kappa inter-rater reliability coefficient was calculated on a random 20% of this material. This was highly significant (κ=.845; p<0.001) showing a very high level of agreement between the raters.

Table 2 Raw scores in percentages (number correct/number scorable) on the Function PEPS-C Tasks.

	AI	AO	CI	FI	FO	TI	TO
Group							
WS (n=9)							
Mean	74	82[a]	64	55[1]	85	86[b]	71[a]
SD	18	19	10	17	15	14	14
Minimum	50	56	50	38	57	56	53
Maximum	100	100	81	94	100	100	94
DS (n=9)							
Mean	65[iii]	32[a/x/i]	56[i]	59[i]	56[2/ii]	63[b/i]	38[a/i]
SD	8	19	15	12	30	10	9
Minimum	56	8	38	38	14	44	27
Maximum	81	60	75	75	100	75	54
MA control (n=8)							
Mean	80	93[x]	73*	69	97[2]	84**	56
SD	22	8	9	20	13	16	38
Minimum	44	81	63	38	93	56	19
Maximum	94	100	88	88	100	100	100
CA control (n=8)							
Mean	88[iii]	94[i]	92[2/*]	89[1/i]	98[ii]	98[i/**]	86[i]
SD	19	6	6	13	3	22	20
Minimum	44	81	88	63	94	88	56
Maximum	100	100	100	100	100	100	100

1. PEPS-C = Profiling Elements of Prosody in Speech-Communication; AI = affect input; AO = affect output; CI = chunking input; FI = Focus Input; FO = Focus Output; TI = turn end input; TO = turn end output; WS = Williams syndrome; DS = Down's syndrome

2. The differences between the groups are marked as follows. WS/DS: [a] significance at 0.001, [b] significance at 0.01; WS/CA: [1] significance at 0.001, [2] significance at 0.01; DS/CA: [i] significance at 0.001, [ii] significance at 0.01, [iii] significance at 0.01; DS/MA: [x] significance at 0.001; MA/CA: * significance at 0.001, ** significance at 0.05.

Results

The results from the PEPS-C task are presented in Tables 2 and 3. Table 2 shows the results from the four function tasks; Table 3 shows the results from the two form tasks. The results are presented in percentages correct rather than in raw scores. This was done due to the fact that some participants did not get a score for reasons other than prosodic features, such as inability to produce the required phrase verbatim or giving the wrong lexical items. Therefore, a percentage correct rather than raw scores was deemed more representative of the participants' prosodic ability.

The data were analyzed using a One-Way ANOVA with posthoc Bonferroni comparisons if the variance was homogeneous (Affect Input, Chunking Input and Focus Input) or Tamhane's comparisons if the variance was non-homogeneous, which was the case for all the remaining variables. The results from the Chunking output task are not presented here because 7 out of 9 participants in the DS group were unable to do this task.

One-Way ANOVA revealed a main effect of group for all aspects of prosody function: Affect Input [$F_{(3,30)}$=3.993, p=0.046], Affect Output [$F_{(3,30)}$=35,434, p=0.000], Chunking Input [$F_{(3,29)}$ = 19,752, p=0.000], Focus Input [$F_{(3,27)}$=9.050, p=0.000], Focus Output [$F_{(3,30)}$=12,791, p=0.000], Turn-end Input [$F_{(3,30)}$ = 14, 761, p=0.000], Turn-end Output [$F_{(3,28)}$ = 8.331, p=0.000]. Post-hoc comparisons revealed the following significant between-group differences: the DS group was significantly poorer than the CA matched group (p=0.04) on the Affect input task, and significantly worse than the WS group (p=0.000), MA matched group (p=0.000) and CA matched group (p=0.000) on the Affect output task. The DS group was also significantly poorer than the CA matched group on the Chunking input task (p=0.000). Also the younger TD children (the MA group) were significantly lower than the older TD children (CA group) on this task (p=0.001). For the Focus input task, the WS group scored significantly lower than the CA group (p=0.000) and so did the DS group (p=0.003). The DS group was significantly lower than the two TD control groups on the Focus output task: MA group (p=0.014) and CA group (p=0.007). The DS group was also significantly lower than the WS group (p=0.002) and CA group (p=0.000) on the Turn-end input task. The MA control group was also significantly lower than the CA control group on this task (p=0.050). The DS group scored significantly lower than the WS group (p=0.000) and the CA group (p=0.001) on the Turn-end output task.

Table 3 shows the results from the PEPS-C form tasks.

Table 3 Raw scores in percentages (number correct/number scorable) on the form PEPS-C Tasks.

	SD	SI	LD	LI
Group				
WS (n=9)				
Mean	78[a]	84[b]	71[b]	70[b]
SD	21	11	25	22
Minimum	50	69	25	34
Maximum	100	97	100	91
DS (n=9)				
Mean	52[a/**/i]	65[b/***/i]	54[b/*/i]	52[b/*/i]
SD	11	18	9	12
Minimum	38	34	38	39
Maximum	69	91	63	73
MA controls (n=8)				
Mean	89[**]	85[***]	89[*]	89[*]
SD	9	19	12	7
Minimum	75	53	69	81
Maximum	100	97	100	97
CA control (n=8)				
Mean	96[i]	98[i]	94[i]	97[i]
SD	6	4	6	5
Minimum	88	91	88	88
Maximum	100	100	100	100

1. PEPS-C = Profiling Elements of Prosody in Speech-Communication; SD = short-item discrimination; SI = short-item imitation; LD = long-item discrimination; LI = long-item imitation; WS = Williams syndrome; DS = Down's syndrome; MA = non-verbal mental age matched controls; CA = chronological age matched controls.
2. The differences between the groups are marked as follows. WS/DS: [a] significance at 0.01, [b] significance at 0.05; DS/CA: [i] significance at 0.001; DS/MA: [*] significance at 0.001, [**] significance at 0.01, [***] significance at 0.05.

One-Way ANOVA revealed a main effect of group for all aspects of prosody form: Short-item discrimination [F (3,30)=14.282, p=0.000], Short-item imitation [F(3,30)=9.859, p=0.000], Long item discrimination [F (3,26) = 13,236, p=0.000], and Long-item imitation [F (3,29) = 18.069, p=0.000]. Post-hoc comparisons revealed the following significant between-group differences: the DS group was significantly poorer than all the other groups on the Short-item discrimination task: DS < WS (p=0.003); DS < MA (p = 0.002) and DS < CA (p = 0.000). The DS group was also significantly poorer than all the three other groups on the Short-item imitation task: DS < WS (p = 0.024), DS < MA (p = 0.014) and DS < CA (0.000). On the Long-item discrimination task, the DS group scored significantly lower than the other three groups: DS < WS (p=0.049); DS < MA (p = 0.001) and DS < CA (p = 0.000). Similarly, on the Long-item imitation task, the DS group scored lower than the other three groups: DS < WS (p=0.044); DS < MA (p = 0.000) and DS < CA (p = 0.000).

Discussion

The chapter's aim was to present data from two clinical populations, children with WS and those with DS, and to compare their performance on a battery of prosodic tasks in order to investigate whether there are any specific prosodic profiles associated with each genetic syndrome. The data analyses revealed that the prosodic profile of the children with DS was different from the prosodic profile of the children with WS. The DS group showed overall poorer performance on all prosody tasks, in particular on the tasks assessing expressive prosody. With regard to prosody function, performance of the children with DS was particularly low on the output task assessing the affective function of prosody. This prosodic function was assessed via a task that required the participant to express likes and dislikes of various types of food items. The children with DS were inconsistent with their production of the prosodic features associated with the expression of likes and dislikes in English, such as use of the rise–fall/fall–rise tone dichotomy modelled in the sample tasks, whereas the children with WS were fairly consistent and better able to be identified by the raters as liking or disliking an item. Thus despite the fact that both clinical populations displayed a comparable level of receptive language and non-verbal abilities, the children with DS showed a significantly lower ability to produce affect intonation. Their average performance was well below chance (on average only 32% of items were correctly identified by the raters) compared to the performance of the individuals with WS, for whom, on average, 80% of items were correctly identified by raters.

Such a finding is in line with the findings of the very first study to compare expressive affective prosody in individuals with DS and those with WS (Reilly et al., 1990), which also reported that individuals with WS spontaneously used more affective prosody than those with DS. The conclusion to be drawn from such findings is that the DS genotype particularly affects the ability to produce the prosodic information used in English to express this particular affective state. This ability seems to be exclusively linked to the DS cognitive profile and does not seem to be related to non-verbal abilities and level of language understanding because, if it had been, we would have expected the WS group to also have difficulties with this skill.

The other intonation function which distinguished between the WS and the DS groups was Turn-end. The participants with WS outperformed the participants with DS on both the input and the output counterparts of the task. The participants with DS had particular difficulty with the output counterpart of the task: on average only 38% of items were correctly identified by the raters suggesting that the children with DS in this study were unable to reliably produce a rising or a falling intonation in order to signal the difference between questions and statements. The children with WS, on the other hand, were not only able to use the two different tones for the purpose of producing a questioning versus declarative intonation but they also, on average, performed better on this task than the typically developing children of a similar level of non-verbal ability.

This last finding is somewhat difficult to interpret in view of the existing literature because, when the pragmatic abilities of these two populations have been compared, few studies have investigated the use of prosody for pragmatic purposes. Even the study by Reilly et al. (1990), which did look into prosody, reported mainly on the use of lexical enrichment devices and no consideration was given to the use of different intonation patterns. Based on data obtained from a parents' and/or teachers' questionnaire, individuals with WS were reported as having poorer pragmatic abilities when compared to individuals with DS in terms of inappropriate initiation of conversations and use of stereotyped conversations (Laws & Bishop, 2004). Laws and Bishop's study, however, did not consider the use of prosody for the purposes of pragmatic meaning. Thus our initial finding, that children with DS may have severe difficulties in situations requiring them to interpret and use questioning versus declarative intonation for the purposes of social interaction, needs further consideration. Similarly, it would be of interest to further investigate the use of prosodic features to signal other pragmatic functions in the two populations.

With regard to prosody form, the children with DS performed significantly lower than children with WS and lower than both TD groups. This applied to expressive and receptive prosody suggesting that when the task involves prosody perception or production without any communicative function, the individuals with DS tend to be weak and perform poorly, suggesting obvious prosodic deficits in this population.

When compared to typically developing children, individuals with WS show prosodic abilities which are similar to those of children matched for mental age and below those of children matched for chronological age. The picture seems different for individuals with DS who seem to have a more varied and generally weaker prosodic profile in that some prosodic abilities seem to be in line with their mental age whereas others, such as expression of affect, understanding and producing questioning versus declarative intonation and prosody form seem to be lower than expected for their mental age. It needs to be pointed out as well that seven out of nine children with DS in this study were unable to perform the chunking output task. This was likely to be due to the task demands; however, this needs to be verified in future research. In addition, spontaneous speech data from individuals with DS are needed in order to investigate whether the prosodic weaknesses which emerged in the elicited tasks would also be evident in spontaneous speech. Our research on WS, for example, has shown that sometimes we get slightly different prosodic profiles with regard to the affective function of prosody in elicited tasks compared to spontaneous speech (Setter et al., 2007).

Conclusion and clinical considerations

Children with WS and those with DS differ with regard to their prosodic abilities, despite having comparable language and non-verbal skills. Notably, children with WS score higher than children with DS on all expressive aspects of prosody under investigation, and in particular on tasks assessing the affect and turn-end prosodic functions. These data point in the direction of the existence of two distinct prosodic profiles, each linked with a specific genetic disorder. In WS, prosodic skills are in line with other cognitive abilities, whereas in DS the prosodic profile is mixed, with severe weaknesses evident in some prosodic domains. The results presented in this chapter are initial observations and based on relatively small sample sizes, and we hope that future research will take these results further in order to unravel the possible reasons of why two clinical populations of similar cognitive abilities have different prosodic profiles. For example, very little is known of whether and in what way the difficulties experienced by individuals with DS with expressive prosody may be linked to their difficulties with segmental phonology. We also do not know whether infants with DS or those with WS use prosodic cues for language acquisition and, indeed, whether prosodic skills in the very early stages of development may be shaping the language profiles of these two populations.

Speech and language therapists working with individuals with WS or those with DS need to consider prosodic skills as part of the speech, language and communication assessment protocols and explore the potential that prosody has on possible remediation of language difficulties. In addition, given that children with DS seem to find it difficult to use prosody for the purposes of expressing affect, which could severely hinder their social communication and interaction with family and friends, an attempt to modify this skill or teach them an alternative strategy to express different feelings may be beneficial. Similarly, the difficulty that individuals with DS have with the understanding and production of questioning versus declarative intonation may lead to misunderstanding and communication breakdown in everyday communication and, therefore, needs to be addressed in speech and language therapy plans. Given that therapy to remediate prosody is often based on modelling and auditory feedback (van Nuffelen, this volume), for which good receptive skills are required, it should be possible to attempt to remediate the difficulties that individuals with DS have with expressive aspects of prosody because they seem to have relatively better receptive prosodic skills.

Acknowledgements

Part of this research was supported by award RES-000-22-1302 from the Economic and Social Sciences Research Council to Vesna Stojanovik and Jane Setter. We would like to thank Laura Wyllie for collecting the data from the participants with Down's syndrome and to Lizet van Ewijk for help with collecting the data from the children with Williams syndrome and from the typically developing controls. We are very grateful to the Williams Syndrome Foundation in the UK, who helped us with the recruitment of the participants with WS, and to DownsEd International, who helped with the recruitment of participants with Down's syndrome. Our warmest thanks extend to all the participants in the study, their parents and teachers and the schools that took part in the study.

References

Bellugi, U., Marks, S., Bihrle, A., & Sabo, H. (1988) Dissociation between language and cognitive function in Williams syndrome. In D. Bishop & K. Mogford (Eds), *Language Development in Exceptional Circumstances* (pp. 177–189). Edinburgh, Scotland: Churchill Livingstone.

Bishop, D. (2003) *Test for the Reception of Grammar.* London: Harcourt Assessment.

Catterall, C., Howard, S., Stojanovik, V., Szczerbinski, M. & Wells, B. (2006). Investigating prosodic ability in Williams Syndrome. *Clinical Linguistics and Phonetics, 20 (7-8),* 531–538.

Chapman, R.S., Schwartz, S.E. & Kay-Raining Bird, E. (1991). Language skills of children and adolescents with Down syndrome: I. Comprehension. *Journal of Speech, Language and Hearing Research, 34,* 1106–1120.

Dodd, B.J. & Thompson, L. (2001). Speech disorder in children with Down syndrome. *Journal of Intellectual Disability Research, 45,* 308–316.

Fowler, A.E. (1990). Language abilities in children with Down syndrome: Evidence for a specific syntactic delay. In D. Cicchetti & M. Beeghly (Eds), *Children with Down Syndrome: A Developmental Perspective* (pp. 302–328). New York: Cambridge University Press.

Fowler, A.E., Gelman, R. & Gleitman, L.R. (1994) The course of language learning in children with Down syndrome. In H. Tager-Flusberg (Ed.), *Constraints on Language Acquisition: Studies of Atypical Children* (pp. 91–140). Hillsdale, NJ: Lawrence Erlbaum Associates.

Frangistakis, J.M., Ewart, A.K., Moris, C.A., Mervis, C.B., Bertr, J., Robinson, B.F. et al. (1996) LIM-kinasehemizygosity implicated in impaired visuospatial constructive cognition. *Cell, 86,* 59–69.

Jarrold, C., Baddeley, A.D. & Hewes, A.K. (1999) Genetically dissociated components of working memory: Evidence from Down's and Williams syndrome. *Neuropsychologia, 37,* 637–651.

Klein, B.P. & Mervis, C.B. (1999) Contrasting patterns of cognitive abilities of 9- and 10-year olds with Williams syndrome or Down syndrome. *Developmental Neuropsychology, 16,* 177–196.

Korenberg, J., Chen, X.-N., Hirota, H., Lai, Z., Bellugi, U., Burian, D. et al. (2000). Genome structure and cognitive map of Williams syndrome. *Journal of Cognitive Neurosciences, 12,* 89–107.

Lacroix, A., Stojanovik, V. Dardier, V. & Laval, V. (2010) Prosodie et syndrome de Williams: Une étude inter-culturelle. *Enfance, 3*, 287–300.

Laws, G. & Bishop, D. (2004). Pragmatic language impairment and social deficits in Williams syndrome: A comparison with Down's syndrome and specific language impairment. *International Journal of Language and Communication Disorders, 39 (1)*, 45–64.

Martínez-Castilla, P. & Peppé, S. (2008) Developing a test of prosodic ability for speakers of Iberian Spanish. *Speech Communication: Special Issue on Iberian Languages, 50*, 900–915.

Martínez-Castilla, P., Sotillo, M. & Campos, R. (2010). Prosodic abilities of Spanish-speaking adolescents and adults with Williams syndrome. *Language and Cognitive Processes, 1/1*: 1–28.

Martínez-Castilla, P., Stojanovik, V., Setter, J. & Sotillo, M. (in press) Prosodic abilities in Spanish and English children with Williams Syndrome: A cross-linguistic study. *Applied Psycholinguistics*.

Nazzi, T., Paterson, S. J. & Karmiloff-Smith, A. (2003) Early word segmentation by infants and toddlers with Williams syndrome. *Infancy, 4*, 251–271.

Peppé, S., McCann, J. & Gibbon, F. (2003) *Profiling Elements of Prosodic Systems – Children (PEPS-C)*. Edinburgh: Queen Margaret University College.

Pettinato, M. & Verhoeven, J. (2009) Production and perception of word stress in children and adolescents with Down syndrome. *Down Syndrome Research and Practice, 13/1*, 48–61.

Prasher, V. & Cunningham, C. (2001) Down syndrome. *Current Opinion in Psychiatry, 14*, 431–436.

Raven, J. (2003) *Coloured Progressive Matrices*. London: Harcourt Publishers.

Reilly, J., Klima, E.S. & Bellugi, U. (1990). Once more with feeling: Affect and language in atypical populations. *Development and Psychopathology, 2*, 367–391.

Rondal, J. (1993). Down syndrome. In D. Bishop & M.K. Mogford (Eds) *Language Development in Exceptional Circumstances* (pp. 165–176). Lawrence Erlbaum Associates.

Rondal, J. & Comblain, A. (1996). Language in adults with Down Syndrome. *Down Syndrome Research and Practice, 4*, 3–14.

Setter, J., Stojanovik, V., van Ewijk, L, & Moreland, M. (2007) The production of speech affect in children with Williams syndrome. *Clinical Linguistics and Phonetics, 9*, 659–672.

Stojanovik, V. (2010) Understanding and production of prosody in children with Williams syndrome: A developmental trajectory approach. *Journal of Neurolinguistics, 23 (2)*, 112–126.

Stojanovik, V (in press) Prosodic deficits in children with Down syndrome. *Journal of Neurolinguistics* (2010), doi: 10.1016/j.jneuroling.2010.01.004.

Stojanovik, V., Setter, J. & van Ewijk, L. (2007) Intonation abilities of children with Williams syndrome: A preliminary investigation. *Journal of Speech, Language and Hearing Research, 50:6*, 1606–1617.

Strømme, P., Bjørnstad, P.G. & Ramstad, K. (2002) Prevalence estimation of Williams syndrome. *Journal of Child Neurology, 17*, 269–271.

Thomas, M.S.C., Annaz, D., Ansari, D., Scerif, G., Jarrold, C. & Karmiloff-Smith, A. (2009) Using developmental trajectories to understand developmental disorders, *Journal of Speech, Language and Hearing Research, 52/2*, 306–320.

Udwin, O. & Yule, W. (1991) A cognitive and behavioural phenotype in Williams syndrome. *Journal of Clinical and Experimental Neuropsychology, 13*, 232–244.

Van Nuffelen, G. (2011). Speech prosody in dysarthria. In V. Stojanovik & J. Setter (this volume) (Eds) *Speech Prosody in Atypical Populations: Assessment and Remediation* (pp. xx–xx). Guildford: J & R Press Ltd.

Wells, B. & Peppé, S. (2001). Intonation within a psycholinguistic framework. In J. Stackhouse and B. Wells (Eds) *Children's Speech and Literacy Difficulties 2: Identification and Intervention* (366–395). London: Whurr.

Appendix

Description of the PEPS-C tasks (also described in Stojanovik et al., 2007; Stojanovik, in press; Martínez-Castilla, Stojanovik, Setter & Sotillo, in press)

Function tasks

Turn-end: This task assesses understanding and production of questioning and declarative intonation. The input task consists of words of food items (e.g., milk) which are presented either with rising or falling intonation. Participants have to decide if the food item has been 'read from a book' (falling intonation) or 'offered' (rising intonation). For the production task participants are asked to produce the words of food items by using the appropriate intonation according to a picture that shows one of the two possibilities (reading or offering).

Affect: This task assesses the ability to identify and express the affect function involved in the intonation distinction of 'liking' versus 'disliking'. In the input task, participants have to identify if the voice on the computer likes or dislikes each food item. In the output task, participants have to produce each food item using the correct intonation for when they like or dislike an item.

Chunking: This task assesses the comprehension and production of ambiguous phrases, which are disambiguated using prosody. In the input task, participants are presented with two pictures that show two possible interpretations of the same lexical items. For example, the utterance *chocolate cake and buns* needs to be interpreted as a cake made of chocolate if the boundary is placed after the second item (/*chocolate-cake/ and buns/*) but as three different food items (/*chocolate/ cake/ and buns/*) if the boundary is placed after the first one. In the output task, participants are presented with only one picture and are asked to say what they see on the picture.

Focus: This task assesses the ability to identify and produce pre-final contrastive stress. In the input task, the participants hear a sentence which stresses one of two coloured socks to express that only one of the socks (the stressed one) was forgotten. Participants have to decide which one has been the forgotten one. For example: '*I wanted BLUE and white socks*' vs. '*I wanted blue and WHITE socks*'. In the output task, participants are presented with a football match between different coloured cows and sheep.

Each time one of the animals has the ball, a commentator gives an erroneous description of the situation in that either the colour or the animal is wrong. For example, for a picture of a blue cow, the commentator says 'the red cow has the ball'. Participants are asked to correct the commentator using pre-final contrastive focus by saying: *No, the BLUE cow has it!*

Form tasks

Short-item and long-item discrimination tasks: These tasks assess the ability to perceive the acoustic prosodic differences involved in the previous functions (the term short-item refers to intonation parameters involved in the Turn-end and Affect tasks while the long-item refers to the prosodic parameters involved in the Chunking and Focus functions). The items in both tasks are laryngograph recordings of the items from the function tasks, which preserve pitch, loudness and length variations but without the lexical information. Participants are presented with pairs of these sounds and they have to decide if the sounds are the same or different.

Short-item and long-item imitation tasks: These tasks assess the ability to imitate different intonation or prosodic forms. Participants have to repeat words/phrases exactly as they hear them. As in the discrimination form tasks, the short-item task contains items from the Turn-end and Affect function tasks and the long-item one from the Chunking and Focus function tasks.

Chapter 3

The role of interactional prosody in language testing activities in Swedish

Christina Samuelsson, Department of Clinical and Experimental Medicine, Division of Logopedics, Linköping University, Sweden

Charlotta Plejert, Department of Culture and Communication, Linköping University, Sweden

Ulrika Nettelbladt, Department of Logopedics, Phoniatrics and Audiology, Clinical sciences, Lund University

Jan Anward, Department of Culture and Communication, Linköping University, Sweden

Introduction

Clinical interaction between speech and language therapists (SLTs) and their clients may consist of different communicative activities (Merrils, 2005). These include sequences of everyday talk, talk-about-talk sequences, language training sequences and language testing activities, and it is reasonable to believe that the prosodic structure of the different activities differs. Samuelsson (2009) demonstrated systematic use of prosody within the setting of speech/language testing. Since SLTs use prosodic features to achieve different goals in language testing and therapy, it is of interest to analyze the prosodic package of different communicative activities within clinical interactions in greater detail. In the present chapter, new data are presented where focus is on a comparison of the prosodic structure of two types of questions occurring in a language testing activity between children with language impairment (LI) and SLTs: questions of a personal nature that open the activity, and questions specific for the language test. It also includes comparisons of prosodic structure between children with LI and children with typically developing language (TL).

Swedish prosody

Prosody may be described as containing the rhythmic, dynamic and melodic features of language. In this chapter, the main focus is intonation, with the acoustic correlate F0 extractions. In intonation, pitch is the most influential prosodic feature. Its reflection in acoustic measures is fundamental frequency, F0, measured in Hz. Fundamental frequency among female speakers has been found to vary between 180 Hz and 400 Hz. The average F0 for women is approximately 220 Hz, and for children approximately 265 Hz (Cruttenden, 1997). However, mean F0 has been shown to decrease throughout childhood; mean F0 for one-year-old children is about 440 Hz and for 12-year-olds about 230 Hz (Wilson, 1987). Furthermore, it has been shown that, at least for reading aloud, the decrease of mean F0 continues with aging for both males and females (Pegoraro Krook, 1988). The results of Pergoraro Krook's (1988) study also indicated that mean F0 is lower for reading than for conversation.

Compared to English, Swedish has a relatively complex prosodic system. It is often referred to as a pitch accent language (Cruttenden, 1997). There are contrasts of vowel quantity, word stress – i.e. initial vs. non-initial stress – as well as of tonal word accents. In Swedish, there are a few hundred minimal pairs distinguished by tonal word accent alone (Elert, 1966), e.g., /t´omtɛn/ - /t`omtɛn/ ('the garden' – 'Santa Claus'). The difference between the tonal word accents is mainly an intonational difference. Accent I patterns of standard Swedish are produced with one pitch peak, although the word has two syllables, whereas the accent II pattern is produced with two pitch peaks in the word. However, the choice of word accent is largely predictable from the morphological structure of the word. Words with monosyllabic stems take accent I and words with disyllabic stems accent II. There is no difference in the degree of prominence between accents I and II. Rather, they are phonological properties of individual word forms. The word accent distinction is also maintained in non-focal position.

Word stress is used in different ways in the languages of the world. Many languages have so-called fixed word stress, e.g., Finnish and Turkish. Swedish uses word stress distinctively in a less predictive way similar to, for example, Russian. In Swedish, a number of minimal pairs can be found where the placement of stress is distinctive: /trˈəmpɛt/ - /trəmpˈeːt/ ('sullenly' –'trumpet'). However, the placement of stress is not the only difference between these words since the quality of both consonants and vowels is affected by stress (Bruce, 1998; Cruttenden, 1997).

Prosodic problems in children with LI

The complexity of its prosody makes Swedish an interesting case for the study of prosodic problems. It has been demonstrated that Swedish children with LI omit unstressed syllables and that they have problems with tonal word accents (Nettelbladt, 1983). In a previous study of prosody in Swedish children with LI, it was shown that as many as 41% of Swedish children with severe language impairment had prosodic problems to some extent (Samuelsson, Scocco & Nettelbladt, 2003). It was also suggested that prosodic problems may be related to the severity of LI, as prosodic abilities significantly correlated with grammatical abilities and language comprehension. Limited prosodic abilities were also related to severe phonological problems. When children with prosodic problems in combination with LI were compared to age-matched controls, the results showed significant differences between the children with LI and the controls with regard to all aspects of prosody under investigation (Samuelsson & Nettelbladt, 2004).

Within this group of children, prosodic problems also occurred in not-so-severe cases of LI. Prosodic problems were grouped according to word, phrase or discourse level; most children had problems at the word and phrase level, and a smaller group had problems predominantly at the discourse level. The results pointed towards a possible differentiation of two separate subgroups; one with prosodic problems primarily related to phonetic and/or linguistic problems, and a second subgroup with prosodic problems at the discourse level, possibly related to interactional problems (Samuelsson, 2004). The most problematic prosodic contrast to acquire for the children with LI was the distinction between the tonal word accents (Samuelsson and Löfqvist, 2005). Since tonal word accents are realized by intonational differences, problems with tonal word accents indicate an intonational problem. This was also the case at the discourse level, where a sub-group of children with LI also had intonational problems (Samuelsson, Nettelbladt & Löfqvist, 2005).

For English speaking children, the prevalence of prosodic problems seems to be significantly lower than for Swedish children. In a study by Wells and Peppé (2003), intonation abilities of English speaking children with language impairments were compared to the intonation abilities of language-matched controls and age-matched controls. No significant differences were found between the LI group and the language-matched control group. However, children with LI scored significantly lower than the age-matched controls regarding some of the investigated aspects of prosody, mainly tasks regarding prosodic output form. This means that the children with LI followed a similar developmental trajectory as typically developing children, but that they showed a significant delay regarding prosodic output form. In the data presented here, all participants included in the study have prosodic problems in addition to their LI.

Clinical interaction

Clinical SLT work comprises a variety of communicative practices. It is reasonable to assume that clinical interactions differ depending on the type of communicative practice clients are engaged in within the session. These differences are also reflected in the prosodic structure of the interaction. Many clinical activities, e.g., training, testing or play, often show a regular pattern of request-response-evaluation (RRE). This pattern also occurs in many other types of adult–child conversation, such as teacher–pupil interaction (Sinclair & Coulthard, 1975). In order to proceed with the activity, participants develop different means to achieve and maintain understanding, sufficient for their mutual purposes. Interaction involving SLTs (and other adults) and children with LI are typically asymmetrical in the sense that the adult often is in charge of the talking, and the child takes few initiatives (Nettelbladt & Hansson, 1993). The conversations between clinicians and children in Nettelbladt's and Hansson's study also exhibited very little syntactic variation. Ridley, Radford and Mahon (2002) carried out sequential analysis of classroom interaction between a child who had problems with language comprehension and her specialist teacher, her mainstream teacher and a peer. The results showed that these conversations mainly followed the RRE structure.

The clinical context of the present study is a language testing situation. The prosodic package of this particular practice has previously been described in a case study (Samuelsson, 2009), where the RRE sequences mainly followed a prosodic structure of questions characterized with rising pitch, answers also characterized with rising pitch and evaluations characterized with a fall. This pattern was also followed by the particular child described in the study. The rationale for conducting the present analysis was to explore whether similar patterns could be found in other comparable interactions with children with and without LI in order to get further knowledge about the assessment of prosody in children with LI. In the previous study, the perceptual impression of the SLP's prosody had many features in common with child-directed speech, such as overall high pitch, large pitch range and stretched syllables. This will be discussed below.

Child-directed speech

It has been shown that prosodic and vocalic properties in infant-directed speech are adapted to the developing child's communicative needs and constraints (Sundberg, 1998). Mothers of newborn babies use higher pitch, produce wider pitch variations and show more prosodic repetitions when speaking to their children than when speaking to adults (Fernald & Simon, 1984). The prosodic pattern of child-directed speech (CDS) has also been shown to be more informative than the prosody of adult-directed speech (Fernald, 1989). Fernald (1989) demonstrated that listeners were able to identify an intended message using only prosodic information to a significantly greater extent in child-directed speech than in adult-directed speech. Prosody is also related to grammatical structure, e.g., regarding phrasal stress and phrasal boundaries. A cross-linguistic comparison highlighted that duration and pitch are reliably associated with boundaries within utterances in both English and Japanese (Fisher & Tokura, 1996). Universal characteristics of language input to infants have been detected and it has been argued that these characteristics facilitate language learning, and caregivers seem to be very consistent across languages with respect to modifications regarding pitch and duration (Kuhl, Andruski, Chistovich, Chistovich et al., 1997). The exaggeration of the phrasal intonation contour may be the most striking prosodic pattern in child-directed speech (Sundberg, 1998).

Sequential analysis

For the present chapter, a detailed sequential analysis was carried out in order to assess the prosodic features of SLTs and of children with and without LI. A sequential analysis of interaction can be made in different ways. In a few earlier studies, Conversation Analysis (CA) has been applied to analyses of children's clinical conversation (Gardner, 2006; Plejert & Samuelsson, 2008; Wells & Corrin, 2003). In CA, understanding and meaning are viewed as collaboratively constructed by participants in interaction and every utterance is analyzed in relation to the context in which it occurs. The present data are analyzed sequentially in a CA-informed way, with a special focus on prosody.

Prosodic analysis

Prosody plays an important role in interaction and it has, by means of CA, proved to be useful, for example, for the display of uptake and reaction (Schegloff, 1998). Intonation also has turn-organizational functions (Couper-Kuhlen & Selting, 1996). Wells and Mcfarlane (1998) describe possible prosodic resources that enable recipients to monitor the course of turn-projection. There is also tentative evidence for a routinized prosodic package in clinical language testing for English and Swedish, despite the different prosodic systems of the two languages (Samuelsson, 2009). How children use prosodic cues in interaction was investigated using CA in a case study of one child in mother–child dyads (Wells & Corrin, 2003). Turn taking, especially the transition relevance place (TRP), was investigated and it was demonstrated that the participants oriented to prosodic patterns in order to identify TRPs (Wells & Corrin, 2003).

There are few studies of children where acoustic analysis of prosody has been carried out. Acoustic measurements of prosody at the discourse level were made in another study by Samuelsson, Nettelbladt and Löfqvist (2005), mainly to illustrate prosodic phenomena identified by a listener's panel.

In the present chapter, a study on interactional prosody of a language testing activity with children with LI is described. The same activity with children without LI is used for comparison. The aim is to describe the prosodic strategies used by SLTs in a language testing activity involving children with prosodic problems as part of their LI. In addition, the children's responses to these strategies are explored. To get as broad a view as possible, the interactions are analyzed both at the group level with acoustic measurements of prosody, and at the individual level with detailed sequential analysis.

Methods and materials

Participants and pre-testing procedures

Seven children with a diagnosis of LI defined in accordance with Swedish clinical practice and with the International Classification of Diseases, ICD-10 were included in the present study. The children were monolingual, with no hearing impairment. Each child with LI and prosodic problems was matched for age, gender and regional dialect with a control child mainly from pre-schools and schools in the same local area as the children with LI. Six different female SLTs participated in the interactions.

Pre-testing included tests of language comprehension, grammatical abilities and oral motor skills. One child scored below age level on language comprehension. With regard to grammatical abilities, three children with LI scored below chronological age level. As regards oral motor skills, no child scored below age level. All control children scored as expected for their age in all aspects of language included in the pre-testing procedure (see Table 1).

In addition to the LI, the children also had prosodic problems as examined with an assessment procedure developed and described in a previous study (Samuelsson, Scocco & Nettelbladt, 2003). For an overview of the assessment procedure see the Appendix.

The results from the pre-testing assessment of prosody showed that all seven children had moderate prosodic problems at the word and discourse level and mild prosodic problems at the phrase level (see Table 2).

Materials

The present data consist of seven test interactions between SLTs and children with LI, seven test interactions between SLTs and children with TL, seven interactions with questions other than test questions between SLTs and children with LI, and between SLTs and children with TL. These interactions constitute the first subtest of the prosodic assessment procedure and comprise the same test questions and the same personal questions, for both the children with LI and their matched controls. The children with LI were recorded at the hospital where they were treated, and the children with TL were recorded at their pre-schools. For both groups of children, a Sony TCS-580V stereo cassette recorder was used and the mouth-to-microphone distance was approximately 50 cm. The recordings were digitized on a PC and analyzed with the speech analysis software Praat (version 4.6.33). Logarithmic F0 extractions were made of key portions of the interactions.

The recordings were transcribed in accordance with the demands of CA, which means that a great variety of detail was taken into account, including pauses, hesitations, overlaps, etc. In the sequential analysis, prosodic features are illustrated by F0-curves of each contribution to the interactions.

Table 1 Age and raw scores on pre-testing for children with LI and their matched controls (best possible result).

Subject		Age		Lang compr (0)		Grammar (56)		Oral motor sk (5)	
LI	C	LI	C	LI	C	LI	C	LI	C
1	C1	5;10	5;8	0	0	54	56	5	5
2	C2	5;6	4;11	2	2	54	56	5	5
3	C3	4;11	4;11	5	3	51	52	5	5
4	C4	4;9	4;9	2	0	43	49	5	5
5	C5	4;10	4;11	15	5	37	48	5	5
6	C6	5;7	5;6	0	0	31	56	5	5
7	C7	7;8	7;9	0	0	56	56	5	5

Table 2 Raw scores of prosodic abilities at word, phrase and discourse level for the children with LI (best possible result).

Child	Word level (48)	Phrase level (26)	Discourse level (0)
1	30	20	3
2	39	21	1
3	31	18	2
4	29	23	1
5	35	20	3
6	23	15	2
7	43	23	3

Results

Group comparisons of prosodic features

An in-depth analysis of prosodic features in all the interactions shows that the mean F0 of the SLTs is high in interactions involving both children with LI and children with TL at 273Hz. The pitch range is also very wide in both groups at 375Hz.

The results also demonstrate that for the therapists the mean F0 is significantly higher in the test questions (p<.001, t=17,93, df=6; see Figure 1), than in the more personal questions when they interact with children with LI. In contrast, the F0 variation for the SLTs, shown by the pitch range, is significantly lower in the test questions (p<.001, t=−7,16, df=5; see Figure 2) than in the more personal questions when they interact with children with LI. This difference between test questions and other questions was not present in the interactions between SLTs and children with TL.

The prosodic pattern described above is followed by the children as regards F0 variation, but not regarding the mean F0. For the children with LI, the mean

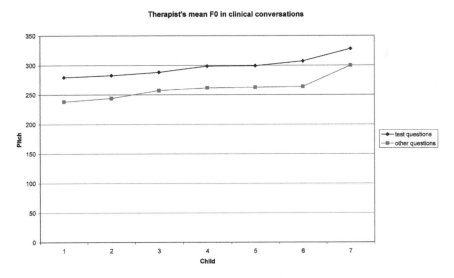

Figure 1 SLT's mean fundamental frequency in interactions involving children with LI.

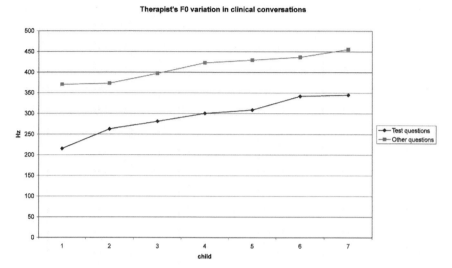

Figure 2 SLT's F0 variation measured by pitch range in interactions involving children with LI

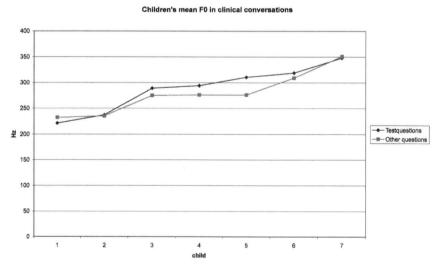

Figure 3 Mean fundamental frequency for children with LI in test questions and more personal questions.

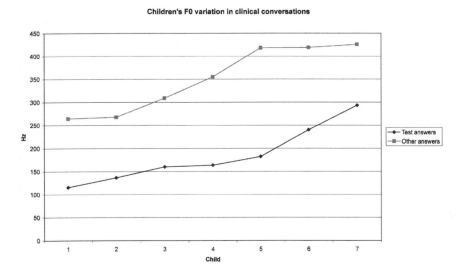

Figure 4 F0-variation measured by pitch range for children with LI.

F0 is fairly similar for the specific test answers and for the other answers in the conversations – M=288Hz and 279Hz respectively (see Figure 3). The F0-variation is significantly lower for the test answers than for the other parts of the conversations, as calculated with a t-test (p<.001, t=–4,69, df=5; see Figure 4). For the children with TL, no difference between test answers and other answers, either for mean F0 or F0 variation, was found. However, it needs to be pointed out that the children's answers are shorter than the SLT's questions. The answers are often only one-word phrases, which makes the pitch variation hard to evaluate.

The comparison of interactions involving children with LI with interactions involving children with TL shows that the therapist's F0 variation, measured as pitch range, is significantly narrower for the test questions in interactions involving children with LI than in interactions with children with TL. The F0 variation of the answers from children with LI is also significantly smaller than the answers from the children with TL. For the other, more personal questions, there is no difference between interactions involving children with LI and interactions involving children with TL.

Example 1

1 SLT: Hur gammal e̲ du Rikard?

How old are you Richard?

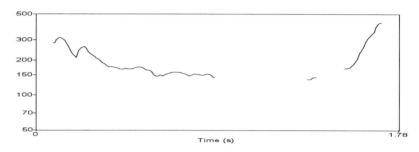

2 R: F̲yra år↑

Four years

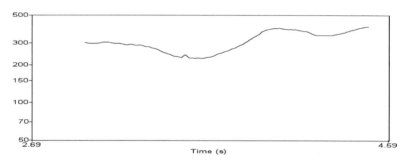

3 SLT: F̲yra år.

Four years.

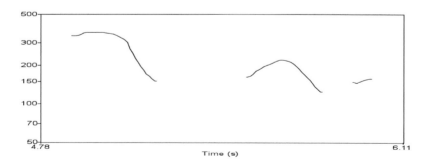

Example 2

1 SLT: Vet du varför man behöver skor?

 Do you know why you need shoes

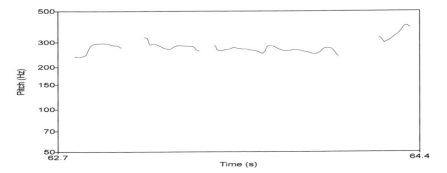

2 C: Ja för man inte ska bli eh (0.3) smutsig.

 Yes, because you should not get eh (0.3) dirty

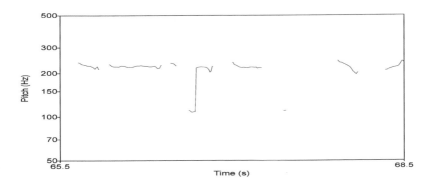

The prosodic structure of the sequential organization

Sequential analysis shows that the language testing activity analyzed in the present chapter mainly follows an RRE structure with requests, responses and evaluations. Prosodically, the structure generally displays a pattern of questions produced with a final rise, responses produced with a rise and evaluations with

Example 3

1 SLT: Vad har du för syskon?

What siblings do you have?

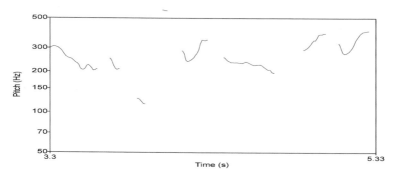

2 C: Vet inte.

Don't know.

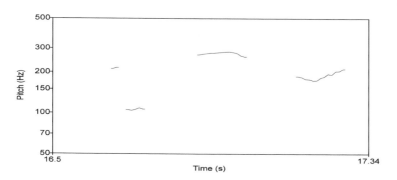

a fall (cf. Example 1). The results at the group level showed that test questions posed to children with LI are produced with a high mean F0 and a small pitch range. At the group level, the children's answers were produced with a high mean F0 and a small pitch range as well. Moreover, this pattern is also present at the individual level. In Example 2, the therapist asks a test question (line 1) with a mean F0 of 279Hz and a pitch range of 177Hz (cf. Example 2). Even though the pitch variation is rather low, the typical final rise is prominent. The child adjusts to this pattern and answers in a fairly high pitch with a slight rise, with

Example 4

1 SLT: Varför ska man inte leka på gatan?

Why shouldn't you play in the street?

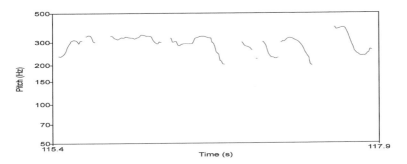

2 C: För det kan komma bilar.

'Cause there may be cars.

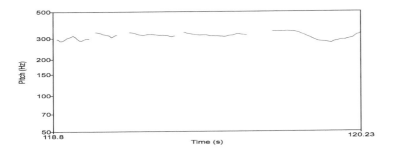

a mean F0 of 222Hz, but with a narrower pitch range than that of the therapist of 88Hz (line 2).

For questions of a personal nature, the results at the group level showed that for children with LI, questions were produced with high pitch. However, the pitch range was wider than for the test questions. This is also displayed at the individual level in Example 3, where the same child as in Example 2 is asked about his siblings. In line 1, the therapist asks the question with high pitch; the mean F0 is 262Hz. The pitch range is 244Hz, which is significantly wider than the pitch range of the previous test question. The child answers in line 2 with

Example 5

1 SLT: Ska du ha kalas på McDonalds när du fyller år?

  Are you going to have a party at McDonalds when you have your birthday?

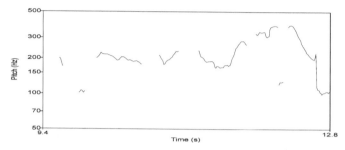

2 C: Ja o lite o ja ska ha o ja ska va eh ha lite kalas hemma först.

  Yes and a little and I shall have and I shall be eh have a small party at home first.

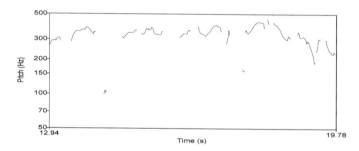

a minimal response with high pitch and a slightly wider pitch range, 111Hz, than in his previous answer.

  The same phenomena are illustrated by Examples 4 and 5, where the therapist in Example 4, line 1, asks a test question with a high mean F0 of 295Hz, and a pitch range of 197Hz. In line 2, the child answers with a mean F0 of 314Hz and a pitch range of 75Hz. In Example 5, the question is regarding a birthday party and the therapist in line 1 asks the question with a mean F0 of 233Hz and a larger variation displayed by the pitch range of 218Hz, which is wider than in the test question. This pattern is mirrored by the child who, in line 2, answers the question in high pitch, 336Hz, with a wide pitch range of 283Hz.

  For children with TL, the difference between test and personal question-answer sequences was not significant at the group level. This was also true for

Example 6

1 SLT: Varför ska man inte leka på gatan?

　　　Why shouldn't you play in the street?

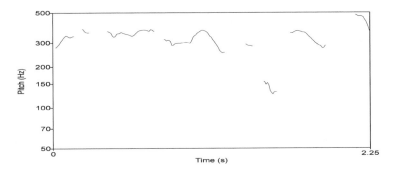

2 C: För att det kommer bilar.

　　'Cause there are cars coming.

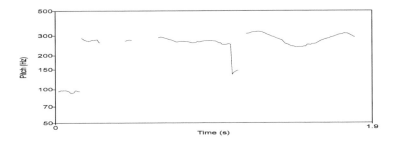

the individual level. In Example 6, line 1, the therapist asks a test question with high pitch of 325Hz and a wide pitch range of 352Hz. The child answers in line 2 with a rather high pitch of 275Hz and a pitch range of 94Hz. The more personal question asked in Example 7, line 1, is also asked with a high pitch of 272Hz and a wide pitch range of 320Hz. The child answers in line 2 with similar mean F0 as in the test question (284Hz) and also a very narrow pitch range of 36Hz. The answer is produced with very low intensity, and the weak second syllable is barely audible.

Example 7

1 SLT: Vet du vad din mamma heter?

   Do you know your mother's name?

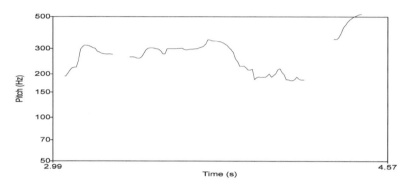

2 C: Lotta

   Lotta

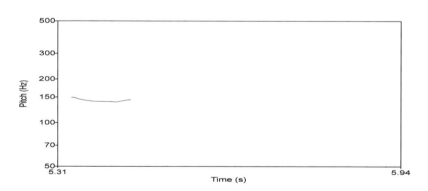

The syntax of the test questions is generally identical since the SLTs follow a script. This is illustrated in Examples 4 and 6, but present in all the interactions. Consequently, the answers also get a certain syntactic and semantic structure, similar for all participating children, as a projection of the questions.

Discussion

The main aim of the present chapter was to describe the prosodic structure of a language testing activity in order to find out whether the SLTs used prosody in a systematic way and, if so, whether the children respond to this pattern in any particular way. In order to get the most comprehensive view possible of the prosody in the interactions, both acoustic measurements and sequential analysis were used. This combination of analytic methods has previously not been used in studies of children with LI.

The results at the group level of the present study demonstrate that, when interacting with a child with LI, the therapists use a particular prosodic package to highlight the specific test questions. This distinction between test questions and questions of a personal nature is not apparent when the SLTs interact with children with TL. The children with LI orient to this pattern by using a similar prosodic pattern as the SLT, even though they have prosodic problems as a part of their LI. Thus, the particular prosodic framing of the activity seems to have a scaffolding effect on the ability to orient to prosodic features which is also evident in children with known prosodic problems. In this task, the children with LI show an ability to imitate prosody, although they have problems imitating other prosodic patterns, e.g., lexical prosody such as tonal word accent patterns, as assessed in formal tests. On the one hand, the imitation of the SLTs' prosody may be a sign of prosodic adjustment, suggesting that the children with prosodic problems are competent contributors in the prosodic co-construction of this type of sequence in interaction. This result stands in contrast to previous findings that showed that for children with prosodic problems, prosodic orientation was problematic (Samuelsson, Löfqvist & Nettelbladt, 2005). Prosodic orientation is defined as one speaker responding prosodically to another speaker's prosody in the immediately following turn (Szczepek, 2001). On the other hand, imitating prosody may also be entirely inappropriate, and the fact that the children imitate the SLTs' prosodic pattern may also be an expression of their prosodic problems, making their prosody odd-sounding at the discourse level.

The mean F0 of the SLTs is high throughout all the interactions. This is also the case for the pitch range, which makes the therapists' contributions to the interactions prosodically similar to child-directed speech. This type of speech has previously proven to interest young infants who focus their speech perception on the phonological properties of spoken language (Sundberg, 1998).

Sequential analysis at the individual level confirms the group level analysis of how prosody is used in interactions. Interestingly, the sequential analysis also contributes with information about syntactic characteristics of the utterances that occur in the activity at hand. Apparently, it is the prosodic package, rather than syntactic structure, that differs between interactions involving children with LI in comparison to children with TL. This finding supports the idea that prosody is used by SLTs as a resource to highlight certain parts of interactions with children with LI.

Conclusions

The results of the present study show that the prosody of the children with LI is influenced by the prosody of the SLT, even when the children are diagnosed with prosodic problems. It is also established that the prosody of the specific test questions is carried out with less varied pitch than question-answer sequences of a personal nature. In addition, detailed analysis shows that the activity is carried out with what appears to be a stereotyped prosodic package. The difference in prosody between the different parts of the testing activity points to the importance of assessing prosody in different activities for children with LI with a particular focus on clinical as well as everyday settings. The results also demonstrate the necessity of raising awareness of prosodic features among speech and language therapists in clinical work.

Acknowledgements

This research has been supported by grants from the Research Council of South East of Sweden (FORSS) and the Swedish Research Council (VR). We would like to thank the children who participated in the study. We would also like to thank their parents and their clinicians for their interest in the study. The procedures followed when carrying out this study were in accordance with the ethical standards of the responsible committee of human experimentation and with the Helsinki Declaration of 1975 as revised in 1983.

References

Bruce, G. (1998) Allmän och svensk prosodi. [General and Swedish prosody] *Praktisk lingvistik, 16.* Institutionen för lingvistik, Lund Universitet.

Couper-Kuhlen, E. & Selting, M. (Eds) (1996) *Prosody in Conversation: Interactional Studies.* Cambridge: Cambridge University Press.

Cruttenden, A. (1997) *Intonation.* New York: University Press.

Elert, C-C. (1966) *General and Swedish phonetics* (in Swedish). Almqvist & Wiksell Förlag AB: Stockholm.

Fernald, A. (1989) Intonation and communicative intent in mothers' speech to infants: Is melody the message? *Child Development, 60,* 1497–1510.

Fernald, A. & Simon, T. (1984) Expanded intonation contours in mother's speech to newborns. *Developmental Psychology, 20,* 104–113.

Fisher C.L. & Tokura, H. (1996) Acoustic cues to grammatical structure in infant-directed speech: Cross-linguistic evidence. *Child Development, 67,* 3192–3218.

Gardner, H. (2006) Training others in the art of therapy for speech sound disorders: An interactional approach. *Child Language Teaching and Therapy, 22 (1),* 27–46.

Kuhl, P.K., Andruski, J.E., Chistovich, I.A., Chistovich, L.A., Kozhevnikova, E.V., Ryskina, V.L., Stolyarova, E.L., Sundberg, U. & Lacerda, F. (1997) Cross-language analysis of phonetic units in language addressed to infants. *Science, 277,* 684–686.

Merrils, D. (2005) *How using a model of therapy interaction can help Speech and Language Therapists talk to children about talking while practicing talking.* Paper presented at the Training the Health Professions: Applying interaction research in health educational settings, University of Southern Denmark, Odense, Faculty of Health Sciences and Institute of Language and Communication, Denmark, October

Nettelbladt, U. (1983) Developmental studies of dysphonology in children. PhD Dissertation. Lund, Sweden: Liber.

Nettelbladt, U. & Hansson, K. (1993) Parents, peers and professionals in interaction with language impaired children. In *Proceedings of the Child Language Seminar 1993* (pp. 219–237). Plymouth: University of Plymouth.

Pegoraro Krook, M.I. (1988) Speaking fundamental frequency characteristics of normal Swedish subjects obtained by glottal frequency analysis. *Folia Phoniatrica, 40,* 82–90.

Plejert, L. & Samuelsson, C. (2008) Recycling in clinical interaction involving children with and without language impairment *Communication and Medicine, 5(2),* 69–80.

Ridley, J., Radford, J. & Mahon, M. (2002) How do teachers manage topic and repair? *Child Language Teaching and Therapy, 18(1)*, 43–58.

Samuelsson, C. (2004) Prosody in Swedish children with language impairment: Perceptual, acoustic and interactional aspects. Ph.D. dissertation, Lunds Universitet (Sweden), Sweden. Retrieved November 7, 2010, from Dissertations & Theses: A&I.(Publication No. AAT C818539).

Samuelsson, C. (2009) Using conversation analysis to study prosodic problems in a child with language impairment. *Child Language Teaching and Therapy, 25 (1)*, 35–64.

Samuelsson, C., Scocco, C. & Nettelbladt, U. (2003) Towards assessment of prosodic abilities in Swedish children with language impairment. *Logopedics Phoniatrics Vocology, 28*, 156–166.

Samuelsson, C. & Nettelbladt, U. (2004) Prosodic problems in Swedish children with language impairment: Towards a classification of subgroups. *International Journal of Language and Communication Disorders, 39(3)*, 325–344.

Samuelsson, C., Nettelbladt, U. & Löfqvist, A. (2005) On the relationship between prosody and pragmatic ability in Swedish children with language impairment. *Child Language Teaching and Therapy, 21(3)*, 279–304.

Samuelsson, C. & Löfqvist, A. (2006) The role of Swedish tonal word accents in children with language impairment. *Clinical Linguistics and Phonetics, 20(4)*, 231–248.

Schegloff, E.A. (1998) Body torque. *Social Research, 65*, 533–596.

Shriberg, L.D. & Kwiatkovski, J. (1982) Phonological disorders III: A procedure for assessing severity of involvement. *Journal of Speech and Hearing Disorders, 47*, 256–271.

Sinclair, J. & Coulthard, M. (1975) *Towards an Analysis of Discourse*. Oxford: Oxford University Press.

Sundberg, U. (1998) Mother tongue – phonetic aspects of infant-directed speech. Ph.D. Dissertation. Stockholm, Sweden: University of Stockholm.

Szczepek, B. (2001) Prosodic orientation in spoken interaction. Interaction and Linguistic Structures, No. 27, November 2001, URL: <http://www.uni-potsdam. de/u/inlist/issues/27/

Wells, B. & Macfarlane, S. (1998) Prosody as an interactional resource: Turn-projection and overlap. *Language and Speech, 41(3–4)*, 265–294.

Wells, B. & Peppé, S. (2003) Intonation abilities of children with speech and language impairments. *Journal of Speech, Language and Hearing Research, 46(1)*, 5–20.

Wells, B. & Corrin, J. (2003) Prosodic resources, turn-taking and overlap in children's talk-in-interaction. In E. Couper-Kuhlen & C. Ford (Eds) *Sound Patterns in Interaction.* Amsterdam: John Benjamins.

Wilson, D.K. (1987). *Voice Problems of Children*, 3rd ed. Baltimore: Williams & Wilkins.

Appendix

Assessment procedure for prosody
C. Samuelsson and U. Nettelbladt, 1999

> **Subtest 1.** Preliminary conversation. Consists of ten questions and a picture. This Subtest was evaluated perceptually using a rating scale where 0= no prosodic deviance, 1= borderline and 2= obvious prosodic deviance.

> **Subtest 2.** Phonology. Consists of 58 target words: 15 with tonal word accent I, of which 9 has word final stress, 23 words with tonal word accent II, and 20 one-syllable words. This Subtest was assessed in two different ways. One way was to calculate Percentage Consonants Correct, PCC, (Shriberg & Kwiatkovski, 1982). The second kind of assessment was made in terms of an analysis of phonological processes.

> **Subtest 3.** Non-word repetition and imitation of nonsense syllable sequences. Consists of 5 syllable sequences with variable stress, two minimal pairs where the tonal word accent varies, and 12 non-words with different stress and tonal word accent. 2 non-words have 1 syllable, 3 have 2 syllables, 2 have 3 syllables and 5 have 4 syllables. This Subtest was scored for prosodic accuracy and one point was given for correct number of syllables, correct stress placement and correct realisation of tonal word accent. In addition, a number of consonants and vowels correct was calculated.

> **Subtest 4.** Vowel quantity. Consists of 4 pairs of pictures with target words with contrasting vowel quantity. This Subtest was scored with one point for achieved contrast of vowel quantity.

Subtest 5. Word stress. Consists of 3 pairs of pictures with target words with contrasting initial vs. final stress and 3 pairs of pictures with minimal pairs of words with 1 or two syllable words, e.g., /stol – pistol/ [chair-pistol]. This Subtest was scored with one point for achieved contrast of word stress.

Subtest 6. Plural. Consists of 8 pairs of pictures with 8 target words in plural. This Subtest was scored with one point for correct plural morpheme.

Subtest 7. Tonal word accents. Consists of 4 pairs of pictures with target verbs with contrasting tonal word accent in infinitive and present tense and 5 pairs of pictures with minimal pairs of words with contrasting tonal word an accent. This Subtest was scored with one point for achieved contrast of tonal word accent.

Subtest 8. Copula. Consists of 10 pictures with a target phrase containing a copula. This Subtest was scored with one point for produced copula in correct tense.

Subtest 9. Indefinite article – finite form. Consists of 5 pictures with one target phrase with indefinite article and one target phrase with finite form of the noun. This Subtest was scored with one point for correct production of indefinite article or finite form of target noun.

Subtest 10. Verb particle vs. prepositional phrase. Consists of 4 pairs of pictures with target phrases with contrasting stress depending on whether the phrase contains a verb particle or a prepositional phrase. This Subtest was scored with one point for achieved contrast of stress.

Subtest 11. Questions. Consists of a structured conversation with a doll to elicit one w-question and one yes- or no-question. This Subtest was scored with one point for correct production of the target question construction.

Subtest 12. Video-narration. Consists of a video sequence watched twice where the children the second time are supposed to retell the story simultaneously; a sort of on-line narration. This Subtest was evaluated perceptually using a rating scale where 0= no prosodic deviance, 1= borderline and 2= obvious prosodic deviance.

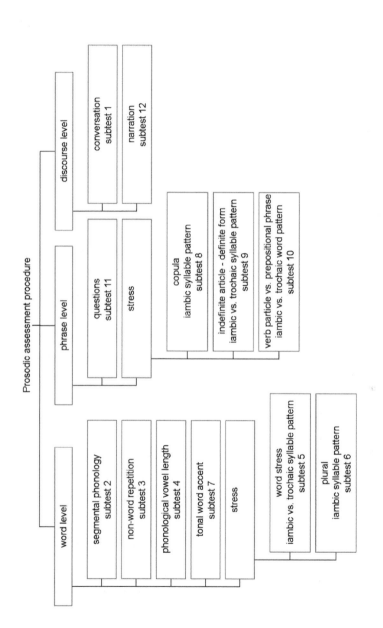

Graphic description of the test procedure.

Chapter 4

The management of turn taking by a child with high-functioning autism: Re-examining atypical prosody

Deborah Kelly, Speech and Language Therapy Department, Warwickshire NHS, UK

Suzanne Beeke, Research Department of Language and Communication, Division of Psychology and Language Sciences, University College London, UK

Introduction

Autism is a neurodevelopmental disorder affecting a child's language, imagination and social skills (Rutter, 2005). Children with high-functioning autism (HFA) have adequate speech for communication and often attend their local school but they experience persisting difficulties with imagination and socialising (Rubin, 2004). One aim of speech and language therapy is to facilitate inclusion for these children. This means more than allowing children access to the curriculum; it also means providing them with the communicative skills needed to access their social networks and communities. These include the ability to initiate, maintain and conclude conversations, skills often reported as atypical in children with HFA (DCM-IV, 1994). Problems using language for the purposes of social interaction result from a number of differences in their speech, language and cognition as compared to typically developing children. One noticeable difference that has received far less attention in the literature is the use of prosody (McCann & Peppé, 2003). Many linguistic studies of prosody have focused on its grammatical functions (e.g., Cruttenden, 1997) and role in expressing emotions (e.g., Bolinger, 1986). More recently, sociolinguistic interest has led to the investigation of prosody's role in interaction or conversation (e.g., Couper-Kuhlen & Selting, 1996).

This chapter will focus on the interactional approach to prosody and its function in a conversation between a 7;11 year-old child with HFA and his mother, in particular in the management of turn endings. Insights from Conversation Analysis (CA) are combined with perceptual prosodic description, and turns of interest are subject to acoustic analysis to support the perceptual data.

This single case analysis will consider the following research questions:

1 How is prosody used in turn taking between a child with HFA and his mother?

2 What are the implications of the findings for intervention that targets the conversational skills of this child?

High functioning autism

Autism is a complex neurodevelopmental disorder, diagnosed around the age of two but thought to be present from birth (Rutter, 2005). Diagnosis involves identifying a triad of impairments – impaired social interaction, limited communication skills, and rigid repetitive stereotypical behaviours – using checklists such as the DSM-IV (American Psychiatric Association, 1994) or ICD-10 (World Health Organization, 1992). The implications of these impairments vary for each individual and, as a result, the disorder is considered on a severity continuum of 'low' and 'high' functioning. Baron Cohen (2000) identifies individuals with autism as high-functioning if they have an IQ in the normal range, and adequate speech and language skills for communication. However, the HFA child's speech and language skills are often delayed at an early age and mild language difficulties may persist. For these children, therapy aims to reduce the impact of social and communication deficits and promote inclusion in everyday social activities with family and peers (Tsatsanis, Foley & Donehower, 2004).

A child with HFA will not show evidence of all features identified by DSM-IV; however, a common feature is 'marked impairment in the ability to initiate or sustain a conversation with others' (criteria 299, DSM-IV, 1994). Conversational management difficulties in HFA have been linked to a number of cognitive theories of autism, such as Theory of Mind (Hale & Tager Flusberg, 2005) and the capacity for shared attention and symbol use (Rubin & Lennon, 2004). However, Perkins (2007) argues that the impairments of these children are not a result of a direct link with an underlying deficit, but are the consequence of one or more compensatory mechanisms motivated by the need to communicate. If this is the case, then any intervention for social interaction skills needs to take into account not only the child with HFA but those with whom he interacts.

Prosodic impairment in autism

Research has demonstrated that prosody is considered atypical in some children diagnosed with HFA (Peppé, Mennen, McCann, Gibbon, O'Hare & Rutherford, 2006). McCann and Peppé (2003: p.327) in their comprehensive review of the literature, reported 'an exaggerated or monotonous intonation, slow syllable-timed speech, a fast rate of speech or an adopted accent different from their peers' to be common features of HFA. They proposed that the resulting conspicuousness of such speech would contribute to difficulties with social acceptance. Despite this, the effects of prosody on the interaction of children with HFA and their family/peers have not been directly researched.

Experimental studies have investigated whether the interactional features of prosody are different in the speech of individuals with HFA. Thurber and Tager-Flusberg (1993) found that individuals with HFA demonstrated typical pausing at phrase boundaries compared to language matched peers, but used fewer within-turn pauses. Conversely, Shriberg, Paul, McSweeney, Klin, Cohen and Volkmar (2001) found increased pausing within turns. Paul, Augustyn, Klin and Volkmar (2005) used Shriberg et al's (2001) data to analyze the relationship between prosodic features and listener perception. They found that features such as stress (defined as intensity, pitch and duration) and resonance (nasality) resulted in listeners scoring speech as atypical. They suggested that remediation methods focusing on prosody needed to 'result in more favourable perceptions on the part of the social partners' (Paul et al., 2005: p.867). In addition they noted the heterogeneity of prosodic features in the speech of the HFA individuals, with variation both in degree and type of prosodic atypicality.

This variability was also noted by Peppé, McCann, Gibbon, O'Hare and Rutherford (2007) in their study using the 'Profiling Elements of Prosodic Systems – Child version' (PEPS–C) (see Chapter 1, this volume). They studied 31 children with HFA aged between 6;01 and 13;06 and found that the understanding of prosody correlated with verbal ability, but that expressive prosodic skills were poorer than predicted by comprehension ability. Given this, the authors suggested that acoustic analysis of the children's expressive prosody was warranted. Diehl, Watson, Bennetto, McDonough and Gunlogson (2008) performed such an acoustic analysis. They found a greater variation in fundamental frequency in 21 children with HFA during narrative tasks than their control group matched on age, IQ and verbal ability, and replicated this with a younger group of 17 children. They cautioned against attributing this directly to the autism, however, as such variation in F_0 is not limited to HFA; children with Williams syndrome have also been found to display the same feature (Setter, Stojanovik, Van Ewijk & Moreland, 2007).

Bellon-Harn, Harn and Watson (2007) in a rare interaction-based therapy study, analyzed the speech in conversation of an 8-year-old with HFA in order to consider expressive prosody in more detail, and develop strategies for intervention. However, their analysis of prosodic strengths and weaknesses was based on samples of the child's speech without reference to the preceding or following talk. Therefore the effects of any 'atypical' prosody on the success of the conversation were not monitored.

In conclusion, studies have tended to analyze the speech of children with HFA out of the conversational context within which it was produced, and have recorded a range of often contradictory findings (see also Ploog, Banerjee & Brooks, 2009). In addition to those applying a predetermined theory-driven approach to elicited data, studies are needed that analyze everyday conversations within which the atypical prosody of HFA may occur, in order to draw conclusions about its functional impact. CA is a methodology that permits such an analysis to be undertaken.

CA: Turn taking and prosody

CA is a method of analyzing talk-in-interaction based on the assumption that conversation is orderly and proceeds on a turn by turn sequential basis (Schegloff, 2007). The seminal model of turn taking (Sacks, Schegloff & Jefferson, 1974) outlines how speakers coordinate overwhelmingly to talk one at a time with little gap or overlap between turns. This is achieved in part because turns display the property of 'projectability', i.e., their end, or transition relevance place (TRP), is signalled by resources including prosody, grammar and eye gaze (Couper-Kuhlen & Selting, 1996). Research has shown that pitch, loudness and duration (Wells & Mcfarlane, 1998; Selting, 2005) and creak (Ogden, 2004) are key prosodic signals of turn ending.

Sacks et al. (1974) suggest that overlap occurs most frequently at possible TRPs, for example when both speakers start talking simultaneously. The majority of overlaps are short and are resolved quickly. There are a number of resolution practices available to participants to repair overlap (Schegloff, 2000). For example, a speaker may drop out to allow the other to continue. If a speaker wishes to hold the floor, they may use phonetic features such as pitch and loudness to signal any overlapping talk as unwelcome (a turn competitive incoming, or TCI). However, Wells and Macfarlane (1998) demonstrated that overlap occurring after a final pitch accent is not treated as turn competitive, i.e., there is a domain of 'acceptable' overlap. Despite this, Wells and Macfarlane (1998) acknowledge that overlap in turn-taking remains rare because a turn is routinely designed to include features prior to the TRP to which potential next speakers orient. Our understanding of the acquisition of such resources by typically developing children is currently limited to a few important studies (Wells & Corrin, 2004; Corrin, Tarplee & Wells, 2001).

Investigating autism using CA

Samuelsson, Nettelbladt and Lofqvist (2005) suggest CA is a useful method for exploring the relationship between aspects of linguistic impairment and problems with social interaction. Radford and Tarplee (2000) explored topic initiation behaviours in the talk of a 10-year-old boy with pragmatic difficulties[3]. The analysis revealed that, despite having typical resources for generating and managing the topic (e.g., topic initial elicitors such as 'what did you do over the weekend'), the boy's conversations resulted in short topic exchanges, in part because he was unable to produce follow-up talk after the partner had responded to his topic enquiry.

Dickerson, Rae, Stribling, Dautenhahn and Werry (2005) used CA to explore the non-verbal resources of gaze and pointing in children with autism. They found that both were used by the children to address a speaker and refer to an object. They argued, therefore, that diagnostic criteria referring to impaired use of non-verbal features in autism need refining.

Local and Wootton (1995) described the phonetic aspects of echolalia while considering what action it served in the conversation of a child with autism and his mother. Their analysis revealed some echolalia was used to maintain the conversational exchange (e.g., to provide an answer to a question) and this

---

3 Pragmatic difficulties are considered crucial to a diagnosis of autism.

was accepted by the mother. However, other examples, referred to as unusual repetitions, were not treated as meaningful by the mother. Analysis of these unusual repetitions revealed a matching of pitch and rate to the mother's prior speech, unlike the other 'acceptable' types of echolalia, which varied in their acoustic features. The authors' findings suggest that, for this child, there are different types of echolalia, and that one type fulfils an interactional function to maintain conversation with his mother.

In summary, it appears that CA has the potential to reveal the contribution of prosody to the management of turn-taking in the talk of children with HFA. In this case study, rather than making an *a priori* assumption that the child will have difficulty taking turns because of atypical prosody, and using this hypothesis to focus the analysis, the authors have used CA as a tool to explore all aspects of turn-taking between the child and his conversation partner. Prosody is viewed as one (extra)linguistic resource amongst many, as a way of ensuring the validity of the findings (Seedhouse, 2005). By exploring the interactional behaviours of both participants, it is hoped that the impact of the child's prosody on turn taking and thus on interaction in general will be revealed.

Method

Case details

Sammy (a pseudonym), 7;11, lives in Warwickshire with his mother and older brother and attends a mainstream school. He has a statement of special educational needs identifying support for autism and speech and language difficulties. He received his diagnosis of autism in 2001 when he was 3;0 from the local team of a paediatrician, a psychologist and a speech and language therapist. A teaching assistant supports him for 30 minutes at the beginning of each school day and during lessons. At the time of this study, programmes for the assistant were provided by the first author, who was his speech and language therapist.

Formal assessment at 7;0 and 7;11 using the Clinical Evaluation of Language Fundamentals – 3rd edition (CELF-3) (Semel, Wiig & Secord, 1995) reveals improvements in both understanding and expressive language skills, although understanding remains below normal limits (see Table 1). Spoken language is characterized by significant word retrieval difficulties. Results suggest that Sammy experiences difficulty with tasks requiring auditory memory and processing when there is absence of visual input. This finding is supported by observation in the classroom. Sammy had a history of speech production difficulties but this had improved significantly by 7;11; substitutions are still evident in unfamiliar words, for example, [mechanic] said as 'mecha<u>m</u>ic', but vowel substitutions are now rare.

The Children's Communication Checklist (CCC-2) (Bishop, 2003) was completed by his mother and teaching assistant at the time of data collection to investigate Sammy's communication and social skills (see Table 1). The checklist asks familiar adults to score how frequently certain communication and social skills occur. Despite his clear diagnosis of autism, the checklist identified Sammy as having language difficulties but not as having a communicative profile characteristic of autism (this would be suggested by a negative social score with a communication score of less than 55). However, his mother reported features that would be consistent with a profile for autism; for example, once or twice a day, Sammy 'seems inattentive, distant or preoccupied with familiar adults' and 'ignores conversational overtures from others'. His teaching assistant commented that many of the examples described in the assessment applied to Sammy in only very specific contexts, and she therefore did not score them as frequent. She judged Sammy's inability to vary his communication skills between situations as occurring 'at least once a week, but not every day'. She reported, however, that when Sammy was in a group without adult support, he was unable to assert himself in the conversation if the children were talking all at once. She queried whether he knew how to join in, and observed that he either became frustrated or lost interest. A number of studies that have used the CCC-2 to differentiate

Table 1 Assessment results for Sammy at Chronological Age (CA) 7;0 – 7;11

Assessment		Chronological age	
		7;00	7;11
CELF–3	Receptive Language	Percentile: 4 Age equivalent: 3;09	Percentile: 13 Age equivalent: 3;11
	Expressive Language	Percentile: 2 Age equivalent: 3;11	Percentile: 19 Age equivalent: 4;09
Reading (School assessment)		Percentile: 80	Percentile: 100
Spelling (School assessment)		Percentile: 90	Percentile: 112
CCC–2	Mother		General communication score: 38 Social deviation score: 6
	Teaching Assistant		General communication score: 54 Social deviation score: 6

children with autism from children with language difficulties have reported overlap between the diagnoses (Bishop & Frazier Norbury, 2002).

A report from Sammy's previous speech and language therapist at age 4;06 identified difficulty with prosody, describing it as 'more noticeable in his longer utterances…he loses fluency and quality in rhythm and intonation'. At 5;03 Sammy's mother felt that his speech remained 'odd' and she was concerned that he stood out from his peers. It is interesting that this was a particular concern for her, given his significant language and pragmatic difficulties at that time.

At the time of video recording (7;11), both Sammy's mother and his classroom assistant reported that his speech sounded better, but remained different from that of his peers. His prosody at this time was described by the first author as:

- Sing-song as a result of pervasive level pitch with sustained vowels in some positions (following Wells & Peppé, 2001)

- Monotone

- Characterized by frequent pauses and extended vowels

- Glottalized

- Creaky and hypernasal.

However, these features were not present at all times. Sammy had a wide prosodic range and was able to vary the loudness of his speech.

Data collection and analysis

A 40-minute video recording was made of Sammy in conversation with his mother at home (the researcher was not present), playing junior scrabble with letter tiles. The data were repeatedly viewed and the talk of both participants transcribed using standard CA conventions (see Appendix 1). Impressionistic phonetic information is provided on the transcribed extracts with pitch contours presented above the talk. The tramlines indicate the top and bottom of the speaker's pitch range. Perceptual analysis has been supported where possible by acoustic analysis using the speech analysis programme PRAAT 4.4.22 (Boersma & Weenink, 2006). Preliminary analysis of turn taking skills revealed patterns of interest around turn transition from Sammy to his mother. These transitions were analyzed in depth in order to identify recurring phenomena in the talk. The data analysis below presents one example of each recurring phenomenon, but reported findings are based on an analysis of all examples of that phenomenon in the data.

Data analysis

The following analysis presents both typical and atypical patterns of turn management in Sammy's conversation with his mother. The first extract has been chosen to demonstrate turn transition in the clear, where Sammy's turn is designed with sufficient prosodic and grammatical resources to project the upcoming TRP and enable smooth transition of talk. Extract 2 shows turn transition that results in overlap of Sammy's ongoing talk by his mother, but is considered typical with reference to the literature (non-competitive overlap). The third extract reveals a pattern of atypical turn transition from Sammy to his mother that involves a problematic overlap and subsequent repair. Finally, Extract 4 reveals another pattern of atypical transition from Sammy to his mother, whereby Sammy takes a turn followed by a pause after which his mother takes a turn, but it transpires that Sammy's turn is incomplete; he has not finished.

Turn transition in the clear

Sammy is able to design turns to enable smooth speaker transition that is either immediate or occurs after a pause of one or two beats. Smooth transition commonly follows Sammy's response to a question, or where Sammy himself has asked a question or made a comment about the game, as in Extract 1.

Extract 1: Prosodic resources for smooth turn-taking

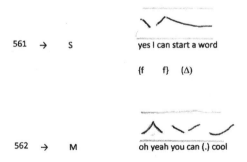

Sammy has just taken some tiles from the bag. In line 561, he initiates a comment on this 'yes I can start a word'. The turn is designed with a cluster of prosodic features to project turn ending, namely a projecting turn ending accent (Wells & Macfarlane, 1998) and a pitch peak (Schegloff, 1998). The comment also signals a TRP by being syntactically complete. Smooth turn transition occurs; his mother responds with no intervening pause (line 562). Interestingly, there is a previous potential syntactic completion point for the turn following 'start' (compare 'yes I can start') but this is not oriented to by his mother. This suggests that Sammy is using resources to project the TRP past this point.

Sammy's turn begins loudly, and an accent is audible on 'can'. The pitch on 'can' rises to mid-height before falling to mid-level on the post-accent syllables 'start a'. There is a very slight final syllable pitch rise. This is illustrated in Figure 1.

There is barely audible creak on 'a' (which cannot be processed, resulting in interruption of the trace); however, the pitch peak on 'can' is clearly evident. Such a pitch peak is suggested by Schegloff (1998) to project a TRP at the next possible point of syntactic completion. Here, this would be after 'start'. However, his mother does not begin her response until the syntactic completion at 'word'. It may be that the accent on 'can' projects past the earlier possible TRP as part of a prosodic pattern that includes more detail than is available in this analysis (Wells & Macfarlane, 1998).

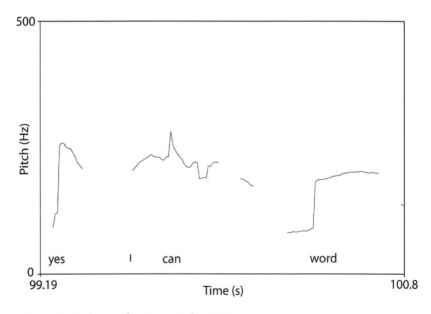

Figure 1: Pitch trace for Extract 4, line 561

In summary, the cluster of prosodic resources in Sammy's turn converges with syntactic completion to project an upcoming TRP to which his mother orients. This and other examples of transition clearly demonstrate that Sammy has typical prosodic resources available to him to successfully project a TRP in his talk.

Typical overlap at turn transition

Overlap occurs in typical conversation but participants work to minimize it. According to Wells and Macfarlane (1998), overlap on post-accent syllables is evidence that a turn has already projected a possible TRP, and participants do not treat this kind of overlap as competitive. Extract 2 presents an example of typical non-competitive overlap (lines 679–680) in Sammy's conversation with his mother. This extract is also noteworthy because it is an example of successful turn-taking despite the presence of additional 'odd' prosodic features in Sammy's turn, namely vowel lengthening and creak.

Extract 2: Non-competitive overlap as evidence of prosodic resources for smooth transition

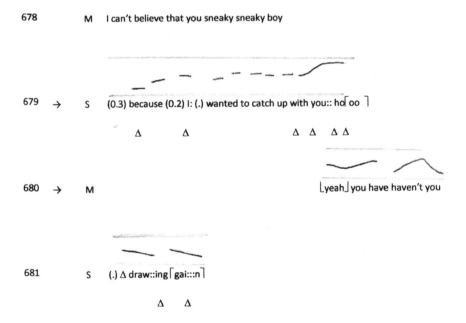

678		M	I can't believe that you sneaky sneaky boy
679	→	S	(0.3) because (0.2) I: (.) wanted to catch up with you:: ho⌈oo ⌉
680	→	M	⌊yeah⌋ you have haven't you
681		S	(.) Δ draw::ing ⌈gai:::n⌉

Sammy has just tricked his mother into playing a tile so he can complete a word and earn a point (see comment, line 678). In line 679, Sammy justifies his behaviour, 'because I wanted to catch up with you' and his mother's response (line 680) is placed as the vowel of his 'you' turns into audible laughter. The TRP after 'catch up with you' is projected via syntactic completion and prosodic resources. An initial accent is audible on 'I' with a fall rise pitch at mid-level, syllable lengthening and creak. This mid-level pitch continues prior to a significant rise on the final accent 'you'. This final accent has a longer duration than the initial accent 'I' and has accompanying creak prior to the audible out breaths that become laughter. Overlap occurs after Sammy finishes saying 'you'. He continues with 'drawing again' (line 681, a reference to taking another tile) once his mother's turn at line 680 has reached a TRP.

If the overlapped incoming at line 680 from Sammy's mother was an attempt to take the floor from him (a turn-competitive incoming), research shows it would have started loud with high pitch (Wells & Macfarlane, 1998). However, there is no audible increase in loudness, and the pitch is falling. The placement of the mother's turn after the final accent in Sammy's talk is within the acceptable domain of non-competitive overlap defined by Wells and Macfarlane (1998).

In this example, a clustering of cues has enabled smooth turn transition to occur despite the presence of additional prosodic features in line 679 which do not appear to serve an interactional purpose, and therefore appear 'odd' in this context. There is vowel lengthening on 'I', which is more usually associated with turn final syllables, although it can be used to hold a turn during overlap (Schegloff, 2006). As 'I' is neither turn final nor produced in overlap, the placement of Sammy's notable vowel lengthening here does not seem to be interactionally motivated, and thus appears atypical. There is also a noticeable amount of creak throughout the turn. However, despite these features, his mother is able to recognize the upcoming TRP, possibly aided in that the atypical vowel lengthening is countered by greater lengthening on the final syllable 'you'.

In summary, the occurrence of non-competitive overlap, of which Extract 2 is one example, adds further support to the argument that Sammy can successfully use prosodic features to project an upcoming turn end. However, there are also examples in the data of overlap resulting from misprojection of the end of Sammy's turn by his mother. These occur around a clustering of features including possible syntactic completion, falling tone, vowel lengthening and audible creak. Such atypical turn transitions can result in problematic overlap and subsequent repair, or in Sammy's mother coming into a pause when it later becomes apparent that Sammy has not finished his turn. These patterns will be demonstrated in Extracts 3 and 4, below.

Atypical turn transition – problematic overlap

This example follows on from Extract 2. Sammy has just tricked his mother into playing a tile so he can complete a word and earn a point, and after justifying his behaviour he comments on the action of taking another tile ('drawing again', line 681).

Extract 3 Misprojection of TRP leading to overlap of Sammy's talk

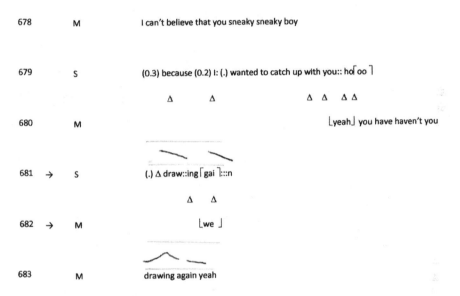

In line 682, his mother's incoming 'we' overlaps Sammy's production of 'again' (pronounced as 'gain', line 681). The prior part of his turn, 'drawing', is potentially syntactically complete and converges with the final syllable feature of vowel lengthening, in this case of 1.0 second, and with audible creak. This is illustrated in Figure 2.

Sammy's mother orients to these pitch features as projecting a TRP, but Sammy continues with 'gain'. Rather than continuing with her turn, his mother cuts off her talk and thus drops out of the overlap. She lets Sammy complete his turn before coming in with a confirmatory repetition of what Sammy said in his overlapped turn ('drawing again yeah', line 683). This overlap and the subsequent interactional work done by the mother to minimize it, and to show that she has understood his full turn, suggest that Sammy's prosodic cues signalled a TRP at a point where he had not finished his turn.

It is worth noting that the mother's abandoned 'we' is possibly a repair of Sammy's omission of a pronoun in line 681. The data do contain evidence to suggest that Sammy's language difficulties prompt his mother to repair such errors. To do this effectively, his mother needs to latch a repair contingently with the error (Ridley, Radford & Mahon 2002). The need to sequentially place her turn next to the error may have converged with the misprojection of a TRP by Sammy to cause the overlap.

Misprojection of a TRP by Sammy can also result in a gap in talk suggesting his mother is unsure whether he has finished his turn or not. In extract 4, Sammy's talk is followed by a pause after which his mother takes a turn but it transpires that Sammy has not finished speaking.

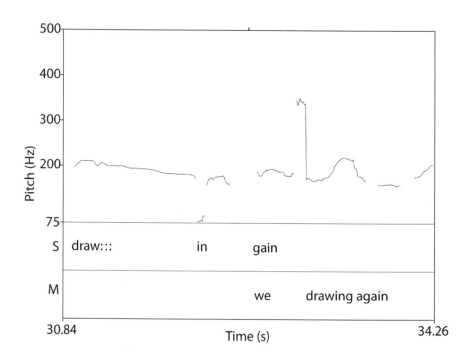

Figure 2 Pitch trace of overlap and repair in Extract 3, lines 681–683.

Atypical turn transition – Sammy's turn appears retrospectively incomplete

Prior to this example, Sammy has completed a word. He begins by commenting on his success by using symbolic noise ('dadada').

Extract 4 Gap in Sammy's talk misprojecting a turn end

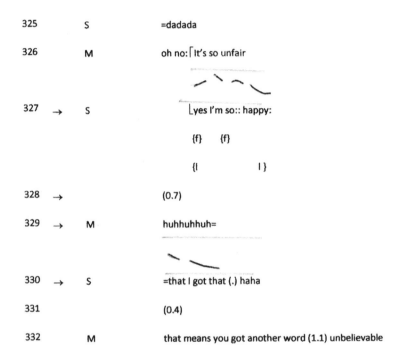

325	S	=dadada
326	M	oh no:⌈It's so unfair
327 →	S	⌊yes I'm so:: happy:
		{f} {f}
		{l l}
328 →		(0.7)
329 →	M	huhhuhhuh=
330 →	S	=that I got that (.) haha
331		(0.4)
332	M	that means you got another word (1.1) unbelievable

In line 327, Sammy overlaps his mother's complaint to say 'yes I'm so happy'. He designs his turn as a (typical) competitive incoming, producing 'yes' with louder and higher pitch than his usual turn starts, evidence he is aware of the need to compete for the floor. A narrow rise-fall on the hearably lengthened final accent 'so' suggests a TRP projecting accent. The falling pitch on the final syllable 'happy' occurs with syllable lengthening, adding to the prosodic resources projecting a turn end. However, the potential TRP is not immediately oriented to by his mother; a 0.7 second lapse in talk occurs before she laughs (line 329). Whilst it is possible, during this lapse, that Sammy's mother is involved in non-verbal game activity that cannot be seen on video, which may be competing for her attention (Wells & Corrin, 2004), she may instead be responding to conflicting cues as to whether or not Sammy intends to continue.

And indeed, despite designing his turn to project a TRP at 'happy', Sammy does go on to expand his turn with the clause, 'that I got that' (line 330). In this interactional environment, one might expect prosodic resources to have projected further talk past the possible TRP following 'happy'. Despite a 0.7 second lapse, the syntactic nature of the additional clause ('that X') strongly suggests that it was designed to be an integral part of the turn at line 327; it appears atypical as a sequentially next turn to the mother's laughter. Thus, the 0.7 second lapse in talk at line 328 appears retrospectively to have been a pause *within* Sammy's turn, and an indication of interactional 'trouble', potentially with turn construction and/or word finding.

In summary, vowel lengthening in positions within turns that appear not to be intended turn endings, combined with within-turn pausing, places Sammy at risk of losing his turn despite the fact that, retrospectively, his intention appears to be to continue.

Discussion

This chapter offers a systematic examination of prosody in the talk of a child with HFA who is considered to have clinically 'odd' prosody. Fine grained analysis of Sammy's turns in sequential context reveals that he can deploy prosody to project the end of a turn. However, there is evidence to suggest that atypical features such as excessive vowel lengthening and creak can miscue turn ending. It is important to note that these atypical features do not always result in turn taking problems.

Sammy's talk displays prosodic features such as pitch movement, vowel lengthening and changes in loudness that are similar to those found in the talk of non-language impaired adults and children (Wells & Macfarlane, 1998; Corrin, Tarplee & Wells, 2001) and he can deploy them at sequentially appropriate places in order to project a TRP or design a turn competitive incoming. The analysis reveals how such prosodic cues converge with grammatical resources to enable Sammy and his mother to manage turn-taking in conversation. Examples show Sammy's mother orienting to pitch movement as one possible resource for projecting the end of turns. This cue proves reliable even when others do not converge, for example, when he elongates vowels. Sammy also uses prosody in a typical way to project past a point of syntactic completion, by maintaining mid-level pitch (Corrin et al., 2001). The analysis reveals that Sammy and his mother are able to use typical resources to pursue their conversation one speaker at a time. Typically functioning prosody is also evident in examples of non-competitive overlap (Wells & Macfarlane, 1998).

However, Sammy's deployment of prosodic resources is not consistent. There are features that appear to prevent smooth transition, including vowel lengthening and creak. When they occur on syllables (retrospectively identifiable as) situated in a mid-turn position, they result in those syllables being treated as turn-final, and overlap occurs. This 'mismatch' between intention to continue talking and prosodic cues results in the disruption of smooth transition.

Another prosodic feature that results in problematic turn transition is pausing. Examples reveal turns designed with pitch movement and final syllable stress converging with points of possible syntactic completion to signal a possible TRP, and followed by a lapse in Sammy's talk. This creates legitimate places for his mother to take the floor. However, as such sequences unfold it becomes clear that Sammy had not in fact finished his turn; what appeared to be a lapse in the conversation can be seen retrospectively to be an intra-turn pause.

It is important to note, however, that vowel lengthening, creak and pausing are also audible in turns where successful transition occurs. These features are part of the 'texture' of Sammy's talk and are audible as such by his mother; analysis here has demonstrated that their presence does not appear to prevent smooth transition in all turn contexts.

This single case study reveals clear evidence of prosodic competency in certain interactional sequences. This is at odds with the findings of much clinical, deficit-focused research. A picture of increased hesitancies, pauses and monosyllabic speech, as determined by perceptual or instrumental analysis (Shriberg et al., 2001; Paul et al., 2005), has resulted in the inclusion of prosodic impairments in diagnostic checklists such as the ICD-10 (WHO, 1992). This study suggests the criteria for identifying prosodic difficulties in children with HFA do not tell the whole story, as highlighted by Dickerson et al. (2005) with respect to non-verbal features of autism. The present study reveals that, for Sammy, typical prosodic features such as a rising pitch on an accent syllable can be employed in combination with other features such as syntactic completion such that they are recognized by a listener as projecting a TRP. Therefore, Sammy is able to manage turn-taking using normal adult-like resources. This presents us with a picture of competency and acknowledges the importance of both participants in using prosody to achieve effective conversation. It also suggests that Sammy does not have a primary disorder of prosody; he is able to signal adult appropriate resources.

However, the picture is not one of complete competency, as Sammy does experience difficulties with turn-taking due to the selection of mismatched cues, particularly where an intra-turn pause is also present. Frequent within-turn pausing is likely to be linked to Sammy's significant word retrieval difficulties, as revealed by formal language testing. It would be interesting to track his prosodic skills in turn-taking in the light of any future improvements in word retrieval difficulties. Future research may profitably consider whether other children with HFA also present with disorders of prosody secondary to their language deficits (Perkins, 2007), and thus whether working on prosody directly is an appropriate target for therapy.

Another potential example of a prosodic anomaly that may result from a behaviour designed to compensate for language impairment is Sammy's use of vowel lengthening. Pausing within a turn places Sammy at risk of losing the conversational floor. To compensate for this, he needs to keep talking and stretching the vowel of the preceding word may be one way to do this. However, vowel lengthening is a typical resource for overlap resolution (Schegloff, 2000). Although it appears to work for Sammy as a compensation for intra-turn pausing on some occasions (Extract 2), in an unexpected sequential context (i.e., *not* during overlap) the strategy can fail to signal continuation past a pause (Extracts 3 and 4). This illustrates the influence that Sammy's conversational partner can have on the development of his talk.

As mentioned earlier, a CA analysis is able to consider all skills available to speakers. However, Sammy's mother's non-verbal responses to his talk were not available for analysis in this video, due to the way she had set up the camera to focus solely on him. In addition, Radford (2009) and others have documented the role of eye gaze and hand gesture in word retrieval. If Sammy's ability to maintain his turn is influenced by his word retrieval difficulties, as is hypothesized here, then this information needs to be included in any future analysis.

Clinical implications

The limitations of a single case study such as this are clear; it is impossible to generalize findings for one child to our knowledge of prosody in HFA as a whole. However, this needs to be balanced against the result of taking together all prosodic behaviours of children with HFA, such as in the experimental studies reviewed above. Although these have revealed much important information about prosody in HFA, individual variation across children's prosodic practices are inevitably washed out when results are grouped. If the aim is to plan intervention, as it was for Sammy, what is happening in conversational interactions at a local level becomes the critical focus.

There have been a number of calls for therapy to correct 'problems of intonation' (see Howlin, 1998), however this is done for the most part by working on prosody out of conversational context (McCann, Peppé, Gibbon, O'Hare & Sutherford, 2005). As this study has shown, a CA methodology enables a clinician to investigate a child's prosodic strengths and weaknesses in context, and to address the conversation partner's behaviours, to identify starting points for a new kind of conversation-focused intervention. To date, there is no precedent for this in the HFA intervention literature; however, there is a growing trend in CA-based interventions for acquired language disorders in adults (particularly aphasia, see for example Beeke, Maxim, Best & Cooper, 2011; Lock, Wilkinson & Bryan, 2001).

Sammy's mother's continued concern at the way he sounded prompted the first author to attempt to take the findings from this study and to develop an intervention programme. Narrowing the focus to turn-taking was seen as more functionally important than narrowing the intervention to a particular prosodic cue such as pausing, and it ensured that other resources, such as grammar, could be considered. Intervention was based on the principles of SPPARC (Lock et al., 2001), a training programme for the conversation partners of adults with aphasia. SPPARC, based on a CA methodology, aims to increase the awareness of patterns within a dyad's own conversation, and to identify and work on strategies for change. The use of video clips from the dyad's own conversations is a key feature of this therapy.

Taking SPPARC as a starting point, a prosodic conversation-based therapy programme was developed that focused on interaction but also incorporated key therapy principles for children with HFA, such as the need for visual and written support. Issues of overlap, pausing and the effects of different types of talk such as question and answer sequences were addressed over four sessions of intervention, using video clips to illustrate behaviours to both Sammy and his mother (see Table 2).

Therapy was evaluated by interviewing Sammy's mother. She reported that it had made her aware of her own adaptations to conversation with Sammy, such as ensuring she had his attention before speaking. Although she had thought she gave him time to finish speaking, she reported now giving Sammy longer to finish his turn, resulting in less overlap and need for repair. Furthermore, she felt that Sammy's overlaps were often as a result of his 'keenness' to speak, rather than an inability to take a turn, and she reported giving Sammy positive

Table 2 Outline of therapy sessions.

Session	Aim
1. What is a conversation?	(a) Introduce features of conversation, including turn taking (see example in Appendix 2)
	(b) Desensitize Sammy to watching himself on video
2. How do we know there's a problem in talk?	(a) Introduce the idea of a problem in talk.
	(b) Problems specific to talk between Sammy and mother demonstrated with transcription from data
	(c) Introduce idea of repairing "problem' in talk
	(d) Mother to monitor gaps and overlap in her talk with Sammy
3. Practising repair	(a) Review homework
	(b) Continue illustration from data how speakers showed problem and how this was overcome
	(c) Practice
4. Wordfinding	(a) Trouble sources of word finding difficulties discussed with Sammy
	(b) Watch video
	(c) Discuss ideas for repairing breakdown
	(d) Practice

reinforcement when he spoke at appropriate points in a conversation, i.e., not in overlap or competition. Interestingly, as the therapy progressed, the mother's focus moved away from how Sammy sounded to how he communicated both with her and with others. She reported her belief that he was more confident in talking to people, and more able to hold his own in conversation.

Although the therapy had attempted to focus specifically on resources used to achieve smooth turn-taking, by taking a functional approach and acknowledging the role of both participants, the therapy appeared to achieve wider changes in overall communicative competence. Unfortunately, there was no opportunity as part of this project to analyze post-therapy talk between Sammy and his mother to see whether her subjective report of improvement was borne out in the data. A next step in the development of this conversation-focused intervention would be a systematic evaluation with multiple linguistic and cognitive baselines, and an objective analysis of change over time in conversation samples.

Conclusion

The management of turn-taking in conversation requires a range of converging grammatical, pragmatic, non-verbal and, of course, prosodic resources, regardless of whether one of the speakers is a child with HFA. This analysis has demonstrated how Sammy's mother orients to prosodic features in Sammy's talk that allow successful transition of turns, and where turn-taking fails, how both of them deploy resources for its repair. Despite the fact that on occasion Sammy's turns display a mismatch of prosodic cues, possibly in an attempt to compensate for his language difficulties, it is encouraging to find that a range of typical prosodic means is available to him in conversation. For this individual child with HFA, atypical features of prosody do seem to be in evidence in conversation, but the overall profile is one of a balance of strengths and weaknesses, rather than merely of overwhelming deficit.

Acknowledgements

We wish to thank Sammy and his mother for participating in this study with such enthusiasm. The work was completed by the first author at University College London in 2006, as part of an MSc in Human Communication.

References

American Psychiatric Association (1994) *Diagnostic and Statistical Manual of Mental Disorders*, 4th ed. Washington, DC: APA.

Baron Cohen, S. (2000) Is Asperger syndrome/high-functioning autism necessarily a disability? *Development and Psychopathology, 12,* 489–500.

Beeke, S., Maxim, J., Best, W. & Cooper, F. (2011). Redesigning therapy for agrammatism: Initial findings from the ongoing evaluation of a conversation-based intervention study. *Journal of Neurolinguistics, 24,* 222–236.

Bellon-Harn, M., Harn, W. & Watson, G. (2007) Targeting prosody in an eight-year-old child with high-functioning autism during an interactive approach to therapy. *Child Language Teaching and Therapy, 23,* 157–179.

Bishop, D.V.M. (2003) *Children's Communication Checklist*, 2nd ed. *(CCC-2)*. Oxford: Harcourt Associates.

Bishop, D.V.M. & Frazier Norbury, C. (2002) Exploring the borderlands of autistic disorder and specific language impairment: A study using standardised diagnostic instruments. *Journal of Child Psychology and Psychiatry, 43,* 917–929.

Boersma, P. & Weenink, D. (2006) PRAAT version 4.4.22. Retrieved from: http://www.praat.org

Bolinger, D. (1986) *Intonation and its Parts*. London: Edward Arnold.

Corrin, C., Tarplee, C. & Wells, B. (2001) Interactional linguistics and language development: A conversation analytic perspective on emergent syntax. In M. Selting & E. Couper-Kuhlen (Eds), *Studies in Interactional Linguistics* (pp. 199–225). Philadelphia: John Benjamins.

Couper-Kuhlen, E. & Selting, M. (1996) Towards an interactional perspective on prosody and a prosodic perspective on interaction. In E. Couper-Kuhlen & M. Selting (Eds), *Prosody in Conversation* (pp. 11–56). Cambridge: Cambridge University Press.

Cruttenden, A. (1997) *Intonation*. Cambridge: Cambridge University Press.

Dickerson, P., Rae, J., Stribling, P., Dautenhahn, K. & Werry, I. (2005) Autistic children's coordination of gaze and talk: Re-examining the 'asocial' autist. In K. Richards & P. Seedhouse (Eds), *Applying Conversation Analysis* (pp. 19–37). Basingstoke: Palgrave Macmillan.

DSIM IV Diagnostic and statistical manual of mental disorders, fourth edition. Diagnostic criteria for 299.00 autistic disorder. (1994). Retrieved from: http://www.togetherforautism.org/articles/autism_symptoms_disorder.php

Diehl, J.J., Watson, D., Benneto, L., McDonough, J. & Gunlogson, J. (2009) An acoustic analysis of prosody in high-functioning autism. *Applied Psycholinguistics, 30*, 385–404.

Hale, C.M. & Tager-Flusberg, H. (2005) Social communication in children with autism. The relationship between theory of mind and discourse development. *Autism, 9*, 157–178.

Howlin, P. (1998). Practitioner review: Psychological and educational treatments for autism. *Journal of Child Psychology and Psychiatry, 39*, 307–322.

Local, J. & Wootton, T. (1995) Interactional and phonetic aspects of immediate echolalia in autism: A case study. *Clinical Linguistics and Phonetics, 9*, 155–184.

Lock, S., Wilkinson, R. & Bryan, K. (2001) *Supporting Partners of People with Aphasia in Relationships and Conversation (SPPARC): A resource pack*. Bicester, UK: Speechmark.

McCann, J. & Peppé, S. (2003). Prosody in autism spectrum disorders: A critical review. *International Journal of Language and Communication Disorders, 38*, 325–350.

McCann, J., Peppé, S., Gibbon, F., O'Hare, A. & Rutherford, M. (2005) Prosodic ability in children with autism. *RCSLT Bulletin, 635,* 14–15.

Ogden, R. (2004) Non-modal voice quality and turn-taking in Finnish. In Couper-Kuhlen, E., & Ford, C., E. (Eds) *Sound Patterns in Interaction: Cross-linguistic Studies from Conversation* (pp 29–62). Philadelphia: John Benjamins.

Paul, R., Augustyn, A., Klin, A. & Volkmar, F.R. (2005) Perception and production of prosody by speakers with autism spectrum disorders. *Journal of Autism and Developmental Disorders, 35,* 205–219.

Peppé, S., Mennen, I., McCann, J., Gibbon, F., O'Hare, A. & Rutherford, M. (2006) Perception of atypical expressive prosody and assessment of prosodic ability in autism spectrum disorders. Paper presented at the 11th Meeting of the International Clinical Phonetics and Linguistics Association, May–June 2006. Dubrovnik: Croatia.

Peppé, S., McCann, J., Gibbon, F., O'Hare A. & Rutherford, M. (2007) Receptive and expressive prosodic ability in children with high-functioning autism. *Journal of Speech, Language and Hearing Research, 50,* 1015 –1028.

Perkins, M.R. (2007) *Pragmatic Impairment.* Cambridge: Cambridge University Press.

Ploog, B.O., Banerjee, S., & Brooks, P.J. (2009) Attention to prosody (intonation) and content in children with autism and in typical children using spoken sentences in a computer game. *Research in Autism Spectrum Disorders, 3,* 743–758.

Radford, J. (2009) Word searches: On the use of verbal and non-verbal resources during classroom talk. *Clinical Linguistics and Phonetics, 23,* 598–610.

Radford, J. & Tarplee, C. (2000) The management of conversational topic by a ten year old child with pragmatic difficulties. *Clinical Linguistics & Phonetics, 14:5,* 387–403.

Ridley, J., Radford, J. & Mahon, M. (2002) How do teachers manage topic and repair? *Child Language Teaching and Therapy, 18: 1,* 43–58.

Rubin, E. (2004). Foreword. *Topics in Language Disorders, 24,* 246–248.

Rubin, E. & Lennon, L. (2004) Challenges in social communication in Asperger syndrome and high-functioning autism. *Topics in Language Disorders, 24,* 271–285.

Rutter, M. (2005) Autism research: Lessons from the past and prospects for the future. *Journal of Autism and Developmental Disorders, 35,* 241–257.

Sacks, H., Schegloff, E.A. & Jefferson, G. (1974) A simplest systematics for the organization of turn-taking for conversation. *Language, 50*, 696–735.

Samuelsson, C., Nettelbladt, U. & Lofqvist, A. (2005) On the relationship between prosody and pragmatic ability in Swedish children with language impairment. *Child Language Teaching and Therapy, 21*, 279–304.

Schegloff, E.A. (1998) Reflections on studying prosody in talk-in-interaction. *Language and Speech, 41*, 235–263.

Schegloff, E.A. (2000) Overlapping talk and the organization of turn-taking for conversation. *Language in Society, 29*, 1–63.

Schegloff, E.A. (2006) Accounts of conduct in interaction: Interruption, overlap and turn-taking. In J.H. Turner (Ed.), *Handbook of Sociological Theory* (pp. 287–322). New York: Plenum Publishers.

Schegloff, E.A. (2007). *Sequence Organization in Interaction: A primer in Conversation Analysis I.* Cambridge: Cambridge University Press.

Seedhouse, P. (2005) Conversation analysis as research methodology. In K. Richards & P. Seedhouse (Eds), *Applying Conversation Analysis* (pp. 251–265). Basingstoke: Palgrave Macmillan.

Semel, E., Wiig, E.H. & Secord, W.A. (1995) *Clinical Evaluation of Language Fundamentals,* 3rd ed. *(CELF- 3).* San Antonio: The Psychological Corporation.

Selting, M. (2005) Syntax and prosody as methods for the construction and identification of turn-constructional units in conversation. In A. Hakulinen & M. Selting (Eds), *Syntax and Lexis in Conversation* (pp. 17–44). Amsterdam: John Benjamins.

Setter, J., Stojanovik, V., Van Ewijk, L. & Moreland, M. (2007) Affective prosody in children with Williams syndrome. *Clinical Linguistics and Phonetics, 21*, 659–672.

Shriberg, L.D., Paul, R., McSweeney, J.L., Klin, A., Cohen, D.J. & Volkmar, F.R. (2001) Speech and prosody characteristics of adolescents and adults with high-functioning autism and Asperger syndrome. *Journal of Speech, Language and Hearing Research, 44*, 1097–1115.

Thurber, C. & Tager-Flusberg, H. (1993) Pauses in the narratives produced by autistic, mentally-retarded, and normal-children as an index of cognitive demand. *Journal of Autism and Developmental Disorders, 23*, 309–322.

Tsatsanis, K.D., Foley, C. & Donehower, C. (2004) Contemporary outcome research and programming guidelines for Asperger syndrome and high-functioning autism. *Topics in Language Disorders, 24,* 249–259.

Wells, B., & Corrin, J. (2004). Prosodic resources, turn-taking and overlap in children's talk-in-interaction. In E. Couper-Kuhlen & C. E. Ford (Eds.), *Sound patterns in interaction: Cross-linguistic studies from conversation* (pp. 119–143). Philadelphia: John Benjamins.

Wells, B. & Macfarlane, S. (1998) Prosody as an interactional resource: Turn-projection and overlap. *Language and Speech, 41,* 265–294.

Wells, B. & Peppé, S. (2001) Intonation within a psycholinguistic framework. In J. Stackhouse & B. Wells (Eds), *Children's Speech and Literacy Difficulties 2: Identification and Intervention* (pp. 366–395). London: Whurr.

World Health Organization (1992) ICD-10 Criteria for childhood autism. International Classification of Mental and Behavioural Disorders. Retrieved from: http://counsellingresource.com/distress/autistic/autism-childhood.html

Appendix 1

Transcription notation

Following the methodology of Wells and Macfarlane (1998), relative pitch height and on-syllable pitch movement are represented impressionistically, above the orthographic transcription, within drawn lines designating the limits of the speaker's normal pitch-range. Additionally, prosodic features such as loudness are shown in brackets {}, which span the amount of speech to which the feature applies.

⌈	a large left-hand bracket links an ongoing utterance with an overlapping
⌊	utterance or non-verbal action at the point where the overlap/simultaneous non-verbal action begins
⌉	a large right-hand bracket marks where overlapping utterances/simultaneous
⌋	non-verbal actions stop overlapping
=	an equals sign marks where there is no interval between adjacent utterances
(.)	a full stop in single brackets indicates an interval of tenth of a second or less in the stream of talk
oh:	a colon indicates an extension of the sound or syllable it follows (more colons prolong the stretch)
°no°	degree signs indicate a passage of talk which is *quieter* than surrounding talk
f	for forte indicates talk delivered at a *louder volume* than surrounding talk
h, heh	indicates discernable aspiration or laughter (the more hs the longer the hah aspiration/laughter)
fu(h)n	h in single brackets marks discernable aspiration or laughter *within* a word in an utterance
°h	discernable inhalation (the more hs the longer the inhalation)

Δ   triangle indicates presence of creak

>talk<   lesser than/greater than signs indicate sections of an utterance delivered at a *greater speed* than the surrounding talk

{l}   for lento indicates the section of the utterance included within the brackets is at a slower *speed* than the surrounding talk

⌈yes   text in double brackets represents a gloss or description of some
⌊((nods)) non-verbal aspect of the talk, and is linked to the relevant section of talk with large brackets (see above)

(1 syllable)
          single brackets containing either a word, phrase, or syllable count (if utterance is very unclear) mark where target item(s) is/are in doubt

------   a broken underline in *bold* indicates speaker's gaze is directed at listener

→   an arrow in *column 2* alerts the reader as to which line contains the issue discussed in the analysis

Appendix 2

Example of worksheet used in conversation-based therapy with Sammy and his mother

So what is a "chat" or "conversation"?

Sender   Receiver/Sender   Receiver

How are you?   Fine thanks.   OK
                          How about you?

Turn 1   Turn 2   Turn 3

It takes two to talk!

Let's look at your conversations with Mum

Turn 1

Turn 2

Turn 3

Part II

Acquired Disorders

Chapter 5

Suprasegmental Aspects of Foreign Accent Syndrome

Jo Verhoeven, Department of Language and Communication Science, City University, London

Peter Mariën, Department of Neurology, Middelheim General Hospital, Antwerp

Introduction

Foreign Accent Syndrome (FAS) is a motor speech disorder in which the speech accent of the patient is perceived by listeners of the same language community as different from the premorbid habitual accent. It is the only motor speech disorder which is defined in perceptual terms. FAS was anecdotally mentioned for the first time in the context of speech and language pathology by the French neurologist Pierre Marie (1907) who reported the case of a male Parisian who developed a different French regional accent (Alsatian) after recovering from anarthria following a left hemisphere stroke. However, he did not explicitly describe the pronunciation characteristics of the speaker that made him sound Alsatian. The second landmark case of a male Czech speaker who developed a Polish accent is reported in Pick (1909). This is the first report of a change in national accent and it is commented that this change is mainly based on the softer articulation of the Czech fricatives (segmentals) and the wrong placement of word stress (suprasegmentals).

Since these early descriptions, about 80 patients with a wide variety of aetiologies have been formally described who presented with FAS either in isolation or, more commonly, in association with other speech and language disorders such as aphasia, apraxia of speech or dysarthria. On the basis of the causal mechanism that triggers the accent change, it is relevant to make a taxonomical distinction between neurogenic FAS, psychogenic FAS and a mixed variant. In *neurogenic FAS*, the accent change is caused by damage to the central nervous system and this type of FAS is by far the most common. In the majority of these patients, FAS results from mostly vascular lesions in the perisylvian speech regions involving the prerolandic motor cortex (BA4), the frontal motor association cortex (BA6 or 44) or the striatum (Dankovicova, Gurd, Marshall, MacMahon, Stuart-Smith & Coleman, 2001). More recently, it has also been shown that the cerebellum may be crucially implicated in the development of FAS (Mariën, Verhoeven, Engelborghs, Rooker, Pickut & De Deyn, 2006; Mariën & Verhoeven, 2007; Cohen, Kurowski, Steven, Blumstein & Pascual-Leone, 2009). Apart from acquired neurogenic FAS, a developmental variant has recently been attested as well (Mariën, Verhoeven, Wackenier, Engelborghs & De Deyn, 2009).

In *psychogenic FAS* there is no evidence of structural brain damage, but the change of accent is deeply rooted in psychological issues of the speaker, such as for instance schizophrenia (Reeves & Norton, 2001; Reeves, Burke & Parker, 2007), conversion disorder (Verhoeven, Mariën, Engelborghs, D'Haenen & De Deyn, 2005; Van Borsel, Janssens & Santens, 2005; Tsuruga, Kobayashi, Hirai & Kato, 2008; Haley, Roth, Helm-Estabrooks & Thiessen, 2009) and bipolar disorder (Poulin, Macoir, Paquet, Fossard & Gagnon, 2007).

Finally, in the *mixed type*, the accent change initially develops as a result of brain damage. The psychological effect of this on the patient is such that the accent is actively further developed in order to sound as a more authentic non-native speaker to reduce the conflict between real and perceived personality (Laures-Gore, Contado Henson, Weismer & Rambow, 2006).

A crucial role in the development of the clinical concept of neurogenic FAS is the seminal paper by the Norwegian neurologist Monrad-Krohn (1947) who reported the case of Astrid L, a 30-year-old Norwegian lady who developed a German/French accent after head trauma caused extensive damage to the left fronto-temporo-parietal region of the brain. According to Monrad-Krohn, the perception of the foreign accent was mainly caused by a change in the speech melody of Astrid L: her speech very often showed rising pitch movements instead of falling movements at the end of utterances. In addition to this, Monrad-Krohn reported that Astrid L initially was not able to implement the Norwegian word accent distinctions correctly. Monrad-Krohn firmly defined FAS as a profound alteration of speech melody (dysprosodia) as opposed to the loss of speech melody (aprosodia). His claim that FAS results from the alteration of speech melody has given rise to a strong clinical focus on prosody and more specifically on intonation in most subsequent case reports.

An extensive review of the literature indeed shows that virtually all papers on neurogenic FAS since Monrad-Krohn (1947) explicitly report problems with speech intonation. Intonation has been variably described as 'strange' (Gurd, Besell, Bladon & Bamford, 1988), 'deviant' (Avila, González, Parcet, & Belloch, 2004), 'abnormal' (Berthier, Ruiz, Massone, Starkstein & Leiguarda, 1991), 'impaired' (Moen, 1990), 'disturbed' (Kwon & Kim, 2006), 'anomalous' (Denes, Trumper, Maddalon & Romito, 1995), 'inappropriate' and 'different' (Cristoph, de Freitas, dos Santos, Lima, Araujo & Carota, 2004). Unfortunately, very few of these statements have been supported by acoustic measurements. In addition, the few studies that did report an acoustic analysis of intonation have yielded contradictory results. In their American patient with an Eastern European accent, Blumstein, Alexander, Ryalls, Katz and Dworetzky (1987) found the use of inappropriate utterance-final rises and unusually large and frequent F0 excursions. Ingram, McCormack and Kennedy (1992) reported an Australian English-speaking patient who developed an Asian/Swedish/German accent. This patient's speech had a quite flat overall F0 and the use of strongly exaggerated phrase-final falls. Moen, Becker, Günther and Berntsen (2007) noted that their speaker was not able to effectively implement the Norwegian word accent distinctions. However, Kurowski, Blumstein and Alexander (1996) found that their speaker's prosody was entirely normal: 'There were appropriate continuation rises at the ends of phrases within sentences as well as appropriate terminal falling contours' (Kurowski et al., 1996: 19). This speaker of American English had developed a Scottish/Irish/Eastern European accent.

The contradictory results regarding the role of intonation in FAS were taken as a starting point for a systematic investigation of the suprasegmental characteristics of the speech of a Belgian patient with neurogenic FAS.

Case report

The patient was a 53-year-old right-handed woman who developed acute speech problems and a right hemiparesis. Her mother tongue is (Belgian) Dutch (Verhoeven, 2005). On presentation at the hospital she was well-oriented, alert and fully cooperative. **Neurological assessment** indicated verbal mutism, intact auditory-verbal comprehension, normal spelling and intact written language comprehension. A moderate right hemiparesis and central facial nerve palsy were found. Sensory examination was normal. No visual field defects or visuo-spatial neglect phenomena were noted. No evidence was found for oral apraxia. Medical history was unremarkable. The patient had worked as a technician in a medical laboratory and had an education level of 14 years. For 10 out of 10 unimanual tasks a strong and consistent right-hand preference was observed

(Oldfield, 1971). On admission, a computerized tomography (CT) scan of the brain was normal. A repeat CT, three days after admission, disclosed an infaction in the left fronto-parietal region. Magnetic resonance imaging (MRI) of the brain confirmed CT findings demonstrating a lesion which involved the inferior frontal gyrus, the precentral gyrus, the anterior insular cortex, the postcentral gyrus and the supramarginal gyrus of the left hemisphere.

Neurocognitive and neurolinguistic examinations were carried out in the acute phase (day 11), the lesion phase (day 27) and late phase of the stroke. **Neurocognitive** investigations were based on a selection of standardized tests. These consisted of: the Mini Mental State Examination (MMSE) (Folstein, Folstein & McHugh, 1975), the Progressive Matrices (Raven, 1938), the Wechsler Adult Intelligence Scale (WAIS) (Wechsler, 1970), subtests of the Hierarchic Dementia Scale (HDS) (Cole and Dastoor, 1987), the Wechsler memory scales (WMS and WMS-R) (Wechsler, 1987), the Rey-Osterrieth figure, the Wisconsin Card Sorting Test (Grant & Berg, 1993), the Right-Left Orientation test, the Visual Form Discrimination test and the Judgment of Line Orientation Test (JLO) (Benton, deS Hamsher, Varney and Spreen, 1983). The neurocognitive test results are summarized in Table 1.

As shown in Table 1, general, verbal and performal intelligence levels, visuo-spatial cognition, orientation, memory, attention, executive functions gnosis and praxis were normal. A slightly depressed score on the performance subtest 'digit symbol substitution' was due to motor slowness as a consequence of a residual paresis of the right arm.

The **neurolinguistic** test battery consisted of a selection of tests including the Dutch version of the Aachener Aphasia Test (AAT) (Graetz, De Bleser & Willmes, 1992), the Boston Diagnostic Aphasia Examination (BDAE) (Goodglass & Kaplan, 1983), the Token Test (De Renzi & Vignolo, 1962), the Boston Naming Test (BNT) (Kaplan, Goodglass & Weintraub, 1983; Mariën, Mampaey, Vervaet, Saerens & De Deyn, 1998), a phonological and semantic verbal fluency task (unpublished norms) and subtests of the Dutch version of the Psycholinguistic Assessments of Language Processing in Aphasia (PALPA) (Bastiaanse, Bosje & Visch-Brink, 1995). Table 2 summarizes the results of the neurolinguistic investigations obtained in the acute phase and lesion phase of the stroke.

Eleven days after admission the patient's oral-verbal output was most markedly characterized by speech apraxia: speech was slowly articulated and hesitant in a slightly hypophonic way. In addition, effortful articulatory struggles, which particularly affected consonant clusters, vowel and consonant prolongations, decreased stress and a general flattening of voice volume gave the impression

Table 1 Lesion phase neurocognitive test results.

Neurogenerative tests	Score/ Maximum	Percentile	Mean	1SD
Mini Mental State Examination	30/30		29	1.3
Intelligence tests				
Wechsler Global IQ (GIQ)	120		100	15
Wechsler Verbal IQ (VIQ)	125		100	15
Information	15/22	93		
Comprehension	18/28	90		
Digit Span	20/24	99		
Arithmetics	11/16	84		
Similarities	20/26	96		
Vocabulary	39/60	82		
Wechsler Performance IQ (PIQ)	110		100	15
Digit Symbol Substitution	36/115	38		
Picture Completion	11/20	73		
Block Design	20/26	93		
Picture Arrangement	19/20	99		
Object Assembly	38/82	66		
Progressive Raven Matrices	125		100	15
Memory tests				
Wechsler Memory Scale-Revised				
Visual Memory Index	>138		100	15
Verbal Memory Index	125		100	15
Delayed Recall Index	>140		100	15
Attention/Concentration Index	112		100	15
Hierarchic Dementia Scale (HDS)				
Memory:Biographic:it. 17	10/10		10	0
Rey-Osterrieth Figure: Memory	34/36		25	3
Frontal tests				
Wisconsin Card Sorting	Normal			
Praxis tests				
Rey-Osterrieth Figure	36/36		35	3
Praxis: Ideational: it. 5 HDS	10/10		9.79	0.17
Praxis: Ideomotor: it 3 HDS	10/10		9.94	0.23
Praxis: Drawing: it. 15 HDS	10/10		9.81	0.52
Praxis: Constructional: it. 12 HDS	10/10		10	0
Visual tests				
Right-Left Orientation – Form A	20/20		19.3	2.3
Judgement of Line Orientation	28/30	22	25.3	
Visual Form Discrimination	30/32		29.9	
Facial Recognition Test	52/54	33-59		

Table 2 Acute phase (day 11) and lesion phase (day 27 post-stroke) neurolinguistic test results.

Aachener Aphasia Test	Results Day 11/27	Percentile	Max	Mean	1SD
Comprehension	**120/120**	**100**	120	108.5	10.24
Auditory: words	30/30	98	30	26.49	3.30
Auditory: sentences	30/30	98	30	26.79	3.41
Total	**60/60**		60	53.28	6.08
Written: words	30/30	95	30	28.30	2.29
Written: sentences	30/30	99	30	26.91	3.39
Total	**60/60**		60	55.21	4.90
Token Test	**0/0**	**100**	60	55.21	4.90
Spontaneous Speech					
Communicative behaviour	**4/4**		5	4.63	0.54
Articulation and prosody	3/3		5	4.63	0.67
Automatisms	5/5		5	4.59	0.65
Semantic structure	5/5		5	4.59	0.53
Phonematic structure	3/3		5	4.54	0.56
Syntactic structure	5/5		5	4.41	0.55
Imposed Speech					
Total repetition	**127/149**	**73/99**	150	144.1	8.07
Phonemes	26/30	50/88	30	28.91	2.09
Monosyllabic words	27/27	50/88	30	28.91	2.09
Loan and foreign words	25/27	52/59	30	28.94	2.31
Compound nouns	24/25	56/76	30	28.45	2.22
Sentences	25/25	59/81	30	28.55	1.90
Total Naming	**120/120**	**100/100**	120	109.3	8.42
Simple nouns	30/30	97	30	27.92	2.90
Colour names	30/30	98	30	27.69	1.99
Composed nouns	30/30	99	30	28.04	2.61
Sentences	30/30	100	30	25.69	3.72
Written Language	**90/90**	**100/100**	90	85.52	7.63
Reading aloud	30/30	96/96	30	28.95	1.93
Composing	30/30	98/98	30	28.57	2.75
Dictational writing	30/30	99/99	30	28	3.67
Boston Naming Test (BNT)	- /56		60	54.5	2.6
PALPA					
Auditory discrimination: test 1	- /70		72	70.05	1.64
Lexical decision: test 5	- /159		160	158.2	2.27
Reading: test 8	- /30		30	29.73	0.67
Repetition: test 8	- /28		30	29.25	1.3

that speech prosody and melody were disrupted. As a result, the perception of speech rhythm was isochronous and scanning.

Though the articulatory distortions affected speech rather inconsistently, errors predominantly consisted of phonemic substitutions. Articulatory groping and struggling (which induced sequential errors) and mostly unsuccessful efforts to self-correction alternated with 'islands of error-free speech'. Errors increased with word length and were not task dependent. No improvement was found when the patient recited, repeated, cursed or read aloud. Aside from this selective impairment of motor speech planning, no accompanying aphasic or dysarthric disturbances were found. As demonstrated in Table 2, auditory-verbal and written comprehension, expressive and receptive syntax, word-finding, written confrontational naming, and dictation writing did not disclose any linguistic deficits.

Neurolinguistic examination in the lesion phase at day 27 after onset of neurological symptoms revealed normal auditory-verbal comprehension and auditory discrimination as illustrated by normal test results on PALPA, Token Test and AAT (Table 2). Spontaneous and imposed oral language examinations were entirely normal. The AAT repetition and visual confrontation naming tests were normal. On the BNT 56 of the 60 items were named correctly. In comparison with a gender, age and education adjusted mean, this score is entirely normal (Mariën, Mampaey, Vervaet, Saerens & de Deyn, 1998). Qualitative analysis of the naming errors according to a classic neurolinguistic taxonomy revealed an error profile that was essentially identical to the profile encountered in a reference group of 200 healthy elderly. The naming errors consisted of adequate circumlocutions of the target item. Verbal fluency for one minute semantic categories (animals, transport, vegetables and clothes) and two minutes phonological categories (phonemes [f], [a] and [s]) matched gender, age and education means (unpublished personal data). All utterances were of normal length and were (morpho) syntactically well-structured.

Though not reflected by formal test results, apraxic speech symptoms disrupted oral verbal output. Inconsistent non-sequential substitutions of target phonemes and phonetic alterations such as prolongations and reductions of speech sounds and diphthongizations characterized spontaneous and imposed speech. Since these articulatory deviations represent phonetic distortions of apraxic origin they were not classified and scored as aphasic errors.

Oral reading, which was contaminated by phonetic alterations, revealed no errors of aphasic origin. Normal AAT results were found at the grapheme, morpheme and textual level. Reading comprehension for words, sentences and texts was within normal limits. The patient was also perfectly able to summarize the contents of a short newspaper article accurately. Dictational writing scored within normal limits on the AAT. The patient obtained a score of 30/30 on dictational writing. Orthography was affected by a residual paresis of the right arm. Tempo was severely reduced and letters were not well-formed.

Perceived accent

The patient and her relatives reported that after the stroke the accent had changed from (Belgian) Dutch to French. This was also the impression of the investigators who heard a clear French accent. In order to objectify this impression, a more formal assessment was carried out by presenting a conversational speech sample to a listening panel consisting of 127 native speakers of Dutch. The speech sample was embedded between a sample of 4 other FAS speakers, 5 speakers with a real foreign accent and 5 native speaker controls. The listeners were asked to freely attribute a perceived accent to each of these samples. From the results it appears that this patient was attributed a French accent by 47.79% of the listeners, while 7.08 heard a German accent. The patient's speech was correctly recognized as (Belgian) Dutch by 37.17% of the participants. Other accents that were assigned were Danish, Eastern European, English, Moroccan and South European (total = 6.94%). It is clear that these results objectify the perception of a French foreign accent in this patient. The segmental characteristics that may have led to the impression that the speaker had a French accent impression have been discussed elsewhere (Mariën & Verhoeven, 2007).

Suprasegmentals

The analysis of the suprasegmental aspects of this speaker's speech was based on a recording that was made in the acute phase of the stroke, i.e., at 11 days post-onset of speech symptoms. This recording consisted of a short informal conversation between the patient and the second author of this chapter. Its duration was 2 min 40 seconds and it consisted of a total number of 206 words. In the first instance, the recording was transcribed orthographically by both authors of this chapter who worked independently of each other. The degree of correspondence between both transcribers was calculated as Cohen's Kappa (Cohen, 1960), which amounted to 1.00: i.e., there was full agreement between both transcribers as to the words that had been said by the patient. Whenever possible, the results of the analyses below are compared with a short speech sample from the patient dating back a few weeks before the stroke: this *pre-stroke* sample consisted of three short prayers which were read in church on the occasion of a wedding anniversary.

Speech rate

Speech rate in the post-stroke speech sample was quantified as speaking rate and articulation rate (Verhoeven, De Pauw & Kloots, 2004). Speaking rate can be expressed as the number of syllables per second (syll/sec) inclusive of pauses and interjections, while articulation rate is expressed as the number of syllables per second excluding pauses. Speaking rate in the post-stroke speech sample was 1.96 syll/sec while articulation rate amounted to 2.80 syll/sec. Both values are considerably lower than the values for Standard Belgian Dutch with a speaking rate of 3.98 syll/sec and an articulation rate of 4.23 syll/sec (Verhoeven et al., 2004). In the patient's pre-stroke speech sample, the average speaking rate was 4.55 syll/sec and articulation rate was 4.65 syll/sec, both values being slightly faster than the reference values for Standard Belgian Dutch.

Rhythm

From a perceptual point of view, it was observed that the patient's speech sounded more syllable-timed and isochronous than the normal stress timing in Standard Belgian Dutch. In order to establish a more objective measure of speech rhythm, a pairwise variability index (PVI) (Low, Grabe & Nolan, 2000) was calculated for the pre-stroke and post-stroke speech samples. This index is based on the idea that durations of vowels in stress-timed languages vary widely while these in syllable-timed languages show less durational variation: this gives rise to a relatively large PVI for stress-timed languages and a relatively small PVI for syllable-timed languages. The PVI for the pre-stroke speech sample was 56.8, while that for the post-stroke speech sample amounted to 44.3. The relatively smaller PVI for the post-stroke speech sample is entirely consistent with the auditory impression of greater syllable-timing in this sample.

Intonation

The patient's intonation was analyzed in two perspectives. On the one hand, several acoustic dimensions of the speaker's utterance F0 were quantified. On the other, the speaker's F0 patterns were analyzed auditorily by means of close copy stylization ('t Hart, Collier & Cohen, 1990).

Acoustic analysis of F0

With respect to the acoustic quantification of the speaker's speech melody, we looked at the speaker's voice compass and her linguistic pitch range. Voice compass is defined in Laver (1994) as '(…) the range of pitch stretching one standard deviation on either side of the mean pitch' (p. 458). This measure provides an indication of the speaker's mean speaking pitch and the F0 range around this mean. This can be considered as a relatively non-linguistic, statistical measure of pitch range. In addition to this, we also looked at the speaker's linguistic pitch range, i.e. '(…) the range within which the phonologically relevant pitch of the speaker's voice habitually varies in paralinguistically unmarked, attitudinally neutral conversation' (Laver, 1994: 457). All measurements were carried out by the standard autocorrelation algorithm in PRAAT (Boersma & Weenink, 2005) which was optimized for intonation analysis.

The analysis of the speaker's voice compass revealed a mean F0 in the speaker's pre-stroke speech of 183 Hz (range = 81.25 Hz), while that in the post-stroke speech sample amounted to 140 Hz (range = 40.67 Hz).

In order to obtain an indication of the speaker's linguistic pitch range, the F0 excursions associated with the sentence accents and continuation rises were measured. For the pre-stroke speech sample the linguistic pitch range was found to be 58 Hz, while that in the post-stroke speech sample amounted to 37 Hz.

Auditory analysis of speech melody

In addition to the measurement of the above-mentioned acoustic dimensions of the speaker's speech melody, an auditory analysis of the intonation patterns was carried out by means of the technique of close-copy stylization which will be defined in more detail below. This technique goes back to the 1970s and 1980s and it was developed by researchers from the Institute of Perception Research, Eindhoven (the Netherlands). Its fundamental aim was to provide a purely phonetic analysis of speech intonation, based as much as possible on the perceptual capabilities of listeners rather than on a number of phonological considerations.

The most fundamental assumption of this approach to the analysis of intonation is that any '(…) F0 curve is a superposition of pitch movements relevant to the perception of speech melody, and of other variations, that are merely ascribable to the irregularities in the oscillation behaviour of the vocal cords' ('t Hart, 1984: 195). Furthermore, at the level of speech production it is argued that '(…) it is unthinkable that all the variations observed are the result of an active neuro-muscular control. Consequently, it would be useless for a speaker to have any conscious intentions to produce them' ('t Hart, 1984: 194).

In the production stage, a distinction can thus be assumed between voluntary and involuntary changes in the periodicity of vocal fold vibration. Voluntary changes result from variations in the states of the laryngeal musculature, insofar as they are actively controlled by a speaker. These changes give rise to gross F0 variations in utterances (macro-intonation). Involuntary changes, on the other hand, fall beyond the speaker's control, since they are determined by other factors. They are primarily dependent '(…) on the air pressure drop across the glottis, and on the accidental height of the larynx, on the position of the tongue and of many other articulators. Therefore, they are dependent on segmental, phoneme-sized aspects ('t Hart, 1979: 62). All these segmental effects are responsible for local perturbations in the F0-curve (micro-intonation).

Given these assumptions, an analysis of intonation can attempt to separate F0 curves into those F0 events which are produced voluntarily and those that are not produced voluntarily, an aim which could be achieved by extracting the discrete command to the laryngeal musculature in the production of speech melody.

From a perceptual perspective, it is furthermore assumed that only voluntarily produced F0 variations are perceivable: '(…) it is counter-intuitive that any speaker intends to produce sounds and sound variations that might not be perceptible ('t Hart, 1984: 195). This assumption makes it possible to analyze F0 curves in terms of F0 variations that are perceivable and those that are not. Only the F0 variations that are produced voluntarily can be expected to be perceivable and relevant to intonation. The detection of perceptually relevant pitch variations was achieved by means of the stylization method.

The *stylization method* basically involves the construction of perceptual analogs to actually observed F0 curves. A stylization can be considered as 'a piecewise linear approximation of an F0 curve with the smallest number of straight line segments that meets the requirement that the synthesized version with this contour is audibly indistinguishable from the resynthesized of the original.' ('t Hart 1986: 1838). A close-copy stylization consequently has to meet two criteria: it should contain the smallest number of pitch movements and at the same time it should be perceptually indistinguishable from the original contour.

In experimental practice, a close-copy stylization is obtained in the following way: the F0 of the utterance to be analyzed is measured and displayed on a

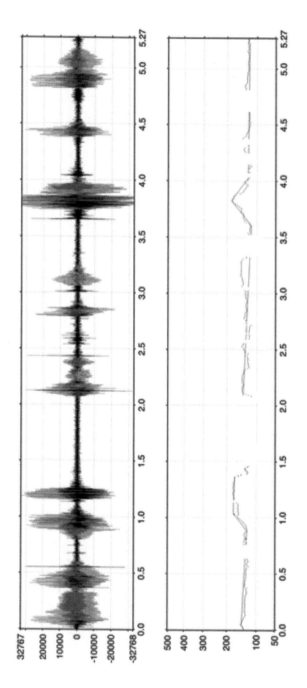

Figure 1 Close-copy stylization of the Dutch utterance 'En dan later ben ik op de grond gevallen' (Gloss: and then later I fell to the ground) as spoken by the patient. The straight lines represent the stylized intonation pattern which consists of a 1-B pattern on 'later' and a 1&A pattern on 'ground'. The dotted line represents the original F0 contour.

screen. Next, the experimenter attempts to make the best possible copy of the original contour. Once this has been achieved, an attempt is made to leave out as much F0 detail as possible, continuously comparing auditorily what the contour sounded like before and after removal of the detail. This effectively involves smoothing out F0 changes and replacing them by straight lines. Thus the experimenter attempts to find a minimal specification which yields the same perceptual impression as the full specification. The result of this method is that the complex F0 curves of utterances are transformed into a sequence of discrete F0 events, the combination of which gives the same melodic impression as the original contours. These events are known as *perceptually relevant pitch movements* and are represented in the stylization as straight line segments. An example of this is given in Figure 1.

The technique was successfully applied to the analysis of various languages such as Dutch (Collier & 't Hart, 1983), English (De Pijper, 1983), German (Appels, 1985) and Russian (Odé, 1989).

In stylizing the F0 curves for this patient, the authors of this chapter worked independently of each other. Subsequently, the stylizations were compared, and where there was any disagreement, a consensus stylization was sought. The stylizations were made by means of GIPOS , which is the original dedicated software developed specifically for this purpose at the former Institute of Perception Research, Eindhoven (the Netherlands), but which is no longer widely available.

On the basis of the stylizations, it was found that the patient used four different intonation patterns which can be regarded as the most elementary contours of Standard Dutch ('t Hart & Collier, 1983). In the first pattern, the sentence accent is realized by means of an accent-lending rising pitch movement (1) which is immediately followed by an accent-lending falling pitch movement (A) on the same syllable. The pitch excursions on the syllable with which they are associated render this syllable more prominent than the others in the same utterance. The general shape of this contour is illustrated in Figure 2.

Figure 2 Illustration of the 1-A intonation pattern which consists of a prominence-lending rise (1) and a prominence lending fall (A) on the accented syllable 'huis'. English gloss: That house is for sale.

This (1-A) intonation pattern occurred 6 times in the post-stroke speech sample and was always associated correctly with the most prominent syllable of the utterance.

An important variant of this elementary contour is the (1-∅-A) pattern, in which the rising and falling pitch movements are associated with two different accented syllables: the two movements are connected by means of a stretch of high declination. The distribution of this contour is restricted to the last two accented syllables in utterances. This contour is illustrated in Figure 3.

Dat **huis** is te **koop**

Figure 3 Illustration of the 1-∅-A intonation pattern which consists of a prominence-lending rise (1) and a prominence lending fall (A) on the accented syllables 'huis' and 'koop'. The two pitch movements are separated by a stretch of high declination. English gloss: That house is for sale.

This contour occurred 11 times in the post-stroke speech sample: in all instances the contour was well-formed and conformed to the distributional requirements.

In another variant of the (1-A) contour, the first accent is realized as a prominence-lending rising pitch movement (1), while the last accent is realized by means of a prominence-lending fall (A). The intervening accents are realized by means of half-falls (E) as a result of which a terraced contour arises. This is illustrated in Figure 4.

Er waren ver**schei**dene **kin**deren **ziek**

Figure 4 Illustration of the 1-E-A intonation pattern which consists of a prominence-lending rise (1) and a prominence lending fall (A) on the accented syllables 'verscheidene' and 'ziek'. The intervening accent 'kinderen' is realised by a half-fall (E). English gloss: Several children were ill.

This contour was used twice by the patient and in both cases the contour was well-formed with respect to the location of the sentence accents.

The last contour was the (1-B) pattern in which the sentence accent is realized by means of a prominence-lending rise (1) after which the pitch remains high.

At some point, the pitch is reset to a lower level to mark a syntactic boundary. This is the standard continuation contour that is used by speakers to indicate that they want to hold on to their speaking turn. This contour is illustrated in Figure 5.

We gaan va**na**vond in ieder geval naar de **schouw**burg

Figure 5 Illustration of the 1-B intonation pattern which consists of a prominence-lending rise (1) on the accented syllable of 'vanavond' and a non-prominence lending fall (B) between 'vanavond' and 'in'. English gloss: In any case we are going to the theatre tonight.

This contour occurred most frequently in the post-stroke speech sample: 35 or 64.48 % of all contours have this shape. A detailed analysis of the contour location reveals that this pattern does not always coincide with major syntactic boundaries, but that it is also used on words within a bigger syntactic unit.

The frequency of the pitch contours used by the patient was compared with frequency information about pitch contours in spontaneously spoken Dutch in Blaauw (1995). On the basis of a perceptual analysis of so-called instruction dialogues of 5 unimpaired native speakers, it was found that the (1-A) contour was most frequent (32.9%), followed by (1-B) which occurred in 19.50% of the cases. (1-E) had an occurrence of 8.39%. In comparison with the frequency of the pitch contours in the post-stroke speech sample there are important differences. In the first instance, the frequency of the (1-B) pattern (64.8%) is extremely high, while the frequency of the (1-A) pattern (11%) is rather low. The frequency of (1-E) (3.70%) is a fraction lower than what can be expected on the basis of the reference information in Blaauw (1995).

Finally, it should be mentioned that all prominence-lending pitch movements were placed correctly by the patient, i.e., on syllables carrying word stress. In addition it has to be noted that all contours conform with the general principle of Dutch intonation that a falling pitch movement has to be preceded by a rising pitch movement. In contrast to other languages, combinations of two falls are not acceptable in Dutch.

Discussion

FAS has traditionally been regarded as a speech disorder that arises from a combination of errors at both the segmental and suprasegmental level. Since

Monrad-Krohn's seminal paper in 1947, the foreign impression of speakers with FAS has widely been associated with deviations in the suprasegmental characteristics of FAS speech. However, these claims have only occasionally been backed up by instrumental measurement. Therefore, it was decided to carry out a systematic instrumental investigation of the suprasegmental characteristics of a (Belgian) Dutch patient who developed a French accent after a left hemisphere stroke (See Appendix 1).

The analysis of speech rate revealed that both the speaking rate and the articulation rate in this patient was slow as compared to the patient's pre-stroke speech as well as to a large Dutch reference sample (Verhoeven et al., 2004). This observation is consistent with the literature in which problems with speech rate are often mentioned (Blumstein et al., 1987; Berthier et al., 1991; Avila et al., 2004; Ardila, Rosselli & Ardila, 1988; González-Álvarez, Parcet-Ibars, Ávila & Gefner-Sclarsky, 2003; Kurowski et al., 1996; Pick, 1919). However, it should be noted that there have also been many patients whose speech rate was explicitly identified as very fluent (Critchley, 1962; Dankovicova et al., 2001; Edwards, Patel & Pople, 2005; Fridriksson, Ryalls, Rorden, Morgan, George & Baylis, 2005; Hall, Anderson, Filley, Newcombe & Hughes, 2003).

The auditory and acoustic analysis of speech rhythm revealed a more syllable-timed speech delivery: the pairwise variability index in the post-stroke speech sample is substantially lower than in the pre-stroke sample (56.8 vs 44.3). This is consistent particularly with Miller et al. (2006) who also reported a lower vocalic PVI in their FAS patient.

The acoustic analysis of intonation revealed that the patient's mean utterance pitch was observed to be substantially lower in the post-stroke speech sample. In addition to this, both non-linguistic and linguistic pitch range were narrower after the stroke. This is indicative of a generally flatter speech melody in the post-stroke speech sample and this agrees well with Ingram et al. (1992).

The auditory analysis of the patient's intonation patterns by means of the stylization method revealed a rather limited inventory of intonation patterns with a remarkably frequent occurrence of the (1-B) pitch contour: this pattern consists of a prominence-lending rising pitch movement on a syllable with sentence stress, followed by a stretch of high declination and terminating in a non-prominence lending pitch reset associated with a syntactic/prosodic boundary. This pattern is typically used by speakers as a continuation marker. The high frequency of this contour in the patient's speech probably reflects a communicative strategy of the patient to keep in charge of the speaking turn. As a result of her slow speech rate and the sometimes long pauses between individual words in utterances, the patient is in constant danger of losing her speaking turn. However, by using the (1-B) intonation pattern the patient indicates that her speaking turn is not finished yet and that there is more information to come. The excessive use of continuation rises has been reported previously by, for instance, Berthier et al. (1991) who reported rising pitch contours at terminal elements and Monrad-Krohn (1947) himself who observed a tendency of 'slightly over-emphasizing and raising the pitch on the last word' (Monrad-Krohn, 1947: 411).

The intonation analysis suggests a flatter speech melody which leaves a monotonous impression and the correct usage of the intonation patterns of Standard Dutch. This conclusion deviates from widespread reports in the literature about abnormal speech melody (Avila et al., 2004; Berthier et al., 1991; Cristoph et al., 2004) and ill-formed intonation patterns (Blumstein et al., 1987; Lippert-Gruener, Weinert, Greisbach, & Wedekind, 2005; Reeves & Norton, 2001) as an inherent feature of FAS. Although FAS is often described as a fundamental 'ataxia of the prosodic faculty' (Monrad-Krohn, 1947: 411), the intonation analysis of this patient shows that this does not necessarily have to be the case and supports earlier claims of normal intonation patterns in Kurowski et al. (1996).

In this patient with isolated neurogenic FAS, who lacked any relevant symptoms indicative of aphasia and dysarthria, no formal linguistic evidence was found to explain the condition in terms of a prosodic disturbance. Absence of such evidence might imply that the presence of subtle deficits at the suprasegmental level in FAS results from an accompanying motor speech or language disorder such as nonfluent aphasia or dysarthria. As a result, thorough linguistic assessments of novel FAS cases are warranted at the diagnostic level to identify the core symptoms of FAS as well as the constellation of speech and language symptoms that may accompany FAS. In addition, the design and implementation of adequate therapeutic interventions for FAS should be motivated by evidence obtained from these in-depth analyses at the neurobehavioural level.

Conclusions

A detailed investigation of the suprasegmental characteristics of a (Belgian) Dutch patient with neurogenic FAS has revealed that, contrary to the view widely-held among speech and language therapists, FAS does not by definition represent a prosodic speech or language disturbance. In addition to a slower speech rate and long pauses, analysis of the patient's post-stroke conversational samples revealed a flatter speech melody leaving a monotonous impression. Although a rather limited inventory of intonation patterns occurred, intonation patterns of Standard Dutch were correctly used. A remarkably frequent occurrence of the (1-B) pitch contour was found, representing a communicative compensation strategy to keep – in the context of a motor speech disorder – in charge of the speaking turn.

References

Appels, R. (1985) A preliminary description of German intonation. *IPO Annual Progress Report, 19*, 36–41.

Ardila, A., Rosselli, M. & Ardila, O. (1988) Foreign accent: an aphasic epiphenomenon? *Aphasiology, 2*, 493–499.

Avila, C., González, J., Parcet, M. & Belloch, V. (2004) Selective alteration of native, but not second language articulation in a patient with foreign accent syndrome. *Clinical Neuroscience and Neuropathology, 15*, 2267–2270.

Bastiaanse, R., Bosje, M. & Visch-Brink, E.G. (1995) *Psycholinguïstische Testbatterij voor de Taalverwerking van Afasiepatiënten (PALPA)*. Hove: Lawrence Erlbaum Associates.

Benton, A.L., deS Hamsher, K., Varney, N.R. & Spreen, O. (1983) *Contributions to Neuropsychological Assessment: A Clinical Manual*. New York: Oxford University Press.

Berthier, M.L., Ruiz, A., Massone, M.I., Starkstein, S.E. & Leiguarda, R.C. (1991) Foreign accent syndrome: Behavioural and anatomical findings in recovered and non-recovered patients. *Aphasiology, 5*, 129–147.

Blaauw, E. (1995) On the perceptual classification of spontaneous and read speech. Utrecht University, OTS Dissertation Series.

Blumstein, S.E., Alexander, P.P., Ryalls, J.H., Katz, W. & Dworetzky, B. (1987) On the nature of the foreign accent syndrome: A case study. *Brain and Language, 31*, 215–244.

Boersma, P. & Weeninck, D. (2005) PRAAT. Doing phonetics by computer [Computer Program]. Version 4.3.27, retrieved 11 October 2005 from http://www.praat.org/

Christoph, D.H., de Freitas, G.R., dos Santos, D.P., Lima, M.A.S.D., Araujo, A.Q.C. & Carota, A. (2004) Different perceived foreign accents in one patient after prerolandic hematoma. *European Neurology, 52,* 198–201.

Cohen, D.A., Kurowski, K., Steven, M.S., Blumstein, S.E. & Pascual-Leone, A. (2009) Paradoxical facilitation: the resolution of foreign accent syndrome after cerebellar stroke. *Neurology, 73,* 566–567.

Cohen, J. (1960) A coefficient for agreement for nominal scales. *Educational and Psychological Measurement, 20,* 37–46.

Cole, M.G. & Dastoor, D.A. (1987) A new hierarchic appproach to the measurement of dementia. *Psychosomatics, 28,* 298–305.

Collier, R. & 't Hart, J. (1983) *Cursus Nederlandse Intonatie.* Leuven: Acco.

Critchley, M. (1962) Regional 'accent', demotic speech and aphasia. In *Livre Jubilaire Docteur Van Bogaert* (pp. 182–191). Bruxelles: L'Imprimerie Des Sciences.

Dankovicova, J., Gurd, J.M., Marshall, J.C., MacMahon, M.K.C., Stuart-Smith, J. & Coleman, J.S. (2001) Aspects of non-native pronunciation in a case of altered accent following stroke. *Clinical Linguistics & Phonetics, 15,* 195–218.

Denes, G., Trumper, J., Maddalon, M. & Romito, L. (1995) Foreign Accent Syndrome: An Italian case study. *Proceedings of the ICPhS95, 2,* 662–665.

De Pijper, N. (1983) *Modelling British English Intonation: An Analysis by Resynthesis of British English Intonation.* Dordrecht: Foris Publications.

De Renzi, E. & Vignolo, L.A. (1962) The token test: A sensitive test to detect receptive disturbances in aphasia. *Brain, 85,* 665–678.

Edwards, R.J., Patel, N.K. & Pople, I.K. (2005) Foreign accent following brain injury: Syndrome or epiphenomenon. *European Neurology, 53,* 87–91.

Fridriksson, J., Ryalls, J., Rorden, C., Morgan, P.S., George, M.S. & Baylis, G.C. (2005) Brain damage and cortical compsensation in foreign accent syndrome. *Neurocase, 11,* 319–324.

Folstein, M., Folstein, S. & McHugh, P. (1975) Mini-mental state: A practical method for grading the cognitive state of patients for the clinician. *Journal of Psychiatric Research, 12,* 189–198.

González-Álvarez, J., Parcet-Ibars, M.A., Ávila, C. & Geffner-Sclarsky, D (2003) Una rara alteración del habla de origen neurológico: el síndrome del acento extranjero. *Revistade Neurología, 36,* 227–234.

Goodglass, H. & Kaplan, E. (1983) *The Assessment of Aphasia and Related Disorders*, 2nd ed. Philadelphia: Lea and Febiger.

Graetz, P., De Bleser, R. & Willmes, K. (1992) *De Akense Afasie Test*. Lisse: Swets & Zeitlinger.

Grant, D.A. & Berg, E.A. (1993) *Wisconsin Card Sorting Test*. Odessa: FL Psychological Assessment Resources.

Gurd, J., Bessell, R.A., Bladon, W. & Bamford, J.M. (1988) A case of foreign accent syndrome, with follow-up clinical, neuropsychological and phonetic descriptions. *Neuropsychology, 26*, 237–251.

Haley, K.L., Roth, H., Helm-Estabrooks, N. & Thiessen, A. (2009) Foreign accent syndrome due to conversion disorder: Phonetic analyses and clinical course. *Journal of Neurolinguistics, 23*, 1–16.

Hall, D.A., Anderson, C.A., Filley, C.M., Newcombe, J. & Hughes, R.L. (2003) A French accent after corpus callosum infact. *Neurology*, 60, 1551.

Ingram, J., McCormack, P. & Kennedy, M. (1992) Phonetic analysis of a case of foreign accent syndrome. *Journal of Phonetics, 20*, 457–474.

Kaplan, E., Goodglass, H. & Weintraub, S. (1983) *The Boston Naming Test*. Philadelphia: Lea and Febiger.

Kurowski, K.M., Blumstein, S.A. & Alexander, M. (1996) The foreign sccent syndrome: A reconsideration. *Brain and Language, 54*, 1–25.

Kwon, M. and Kim, J.S. (2006) A change of dialect after stroke: A variant of foreign accent syndrome. *European Neurology, 56*, 249–252.

Laures-Gore, J., Contado Henson, J., Weismer, G. & Rambow, M. (2006) Two cases of foreign accent syndrome: An acoustic-phonetic description. *Clinical Linguistics & Phonetics, 20*, 781–790.

Laver, J. (1994). *Principles of Phonetics*. Cambridge: CambridgeUniversity Press.

Lippert-Gruener, M., Weinert, U., Greisbach, T. & Wedekind, C. (2005) Foreign accent syndrome following traumatic brain injury. *Brain Injury, 19*, 955–958.

Low, E., Grabe, E. & Nolan, F. (2000). Quantitative characterisation of speech rhythm. *Language and Speech, 43*, 377–401.

Marie, P. (1907). Présentation de malades atteints d'anarthrie par lésion de l'hémisphère guache du cerveau. *Bulletins et Mémoires de la Soc. Méd. Des Hôpitaux, 1*, 158–160.

Mariën, P., Mampaey, E., Vervaet, A., Saerens, J. & De Deyn, P.P. (1998). Normative data for the Boston Naming Test in native Dutch-speaking Belgian elderly. *Brain and Language*, *65*, 447–467.

Mariën, P., Verhoeven, J., Engelborghs, S., Rooker, S., Pickut, B. & De Deyn, P.P. (2006) A role for the cerebellum in motor speech planning: Evidence from Foreign Accent Syndrome. *Clinical Neurology and Neurosurgery*, *108*, 518–522.

Mariën, P. & Verhoeven, J. (2007) Cerebellar involvement in motor speech planning: Some further evidence from Foreign Accent Syndrome. *Folia Phoniatrica et Logopaedica*, *59*, 210–217.

Mariën, P., Verhoeven, J., Wackenier, P., Engelborghs, S. & De Deyn, P.P. (2009) Foreign Accent Syndrome as a developmental motor speech disorder. *Cortex*, *45*, 870–878.

Miller, N., Lowit, A. & O'Sullivan, H. (2006). What makes acquired foreign accent syndrome foreign? *Journal of Neurolinguistics*, *19*: 385–409.

Moen, I. (1990) A case of the 'foreign-accent syndrome'. *Clinical Linguistics & Phonetics*, *4*, 295–302.

Moen, I., Becker, F., Günther, L. & Berntsen, M. (2007) An acoustic investigation of pitch accent contrasts in the speech of a Norwegian patient with the foreign accent syndrome. *Proceedings of the XVIth Congress of Phonetic Sciences*, 2017–2020.

Monrad-Krohn, G.H. (1947) Dysprosody or altered 'melody of language'. *Brain*, *70*, 405–415.

Odé, C. (1989) *Russian Intonation: A Perceptual Description*. Amsterdam: Rodopi.

Oldfield, R.C. (1971) The assessment and analysis of handedness: the Edinburgh Inventory. *Neuropsychologia*, *9*, 97–113.

Pick, A. (1919) Über Änderungen des Sprachcharakters als Begleiterscheinung aphasischer Störungen. *Zeitschrift für die gesamte Neurologie und Psychiatrie*, *XLV*, 230–241.

Poulin, S., Macoir, J., Paquet, N., Fossard, M. & Gagnon, L. (2007). Psychogenic or neurogenic origin of agrammatism and foreign accent syndrome in a bipolar patient: A case report. *Annals of General Psychiatry*, *6*, 1–7.

Raven, J.C. (1938) *Standard Progressive Matrices*. London: H.K. Lewis.

Reeves, R.R. & Norton, J.W. (2001) Foreign accent-like syndrome during psychotic exacerbations. *Neuropsychiatry, Neuropsychology and Behavioral Neurology, 14*, 135–138.

Reeves, R.R., Burke, R. & Parker, J. (2007) Characteristics of psychotic patients with foreign accent syndrome. *Journal of Neuropsychiatry and Clinical Neuroscience, 19*, 70–76.

Tsuruga, K., Kobayashi, T., Hirai, N. & Kato, S. (2008) Foreign accent syndrome in a case of dissociative (conversion) disorder. *Seishin Shinkeigaku Zasshi, 110*, 79–87.

't Hart, J. (1979) Explorations in automatic stylization of F0 curves. *IPO Annual Progress Report, 14*, 61–65.

't Hart, J. (1984) A phonetic approach to intonation: From pitch contours to intonation patterns. In: D. Gibbon & H. Richter (Eds) *Intonation, Accent and Rhythm: Studies in Discourse Phonology*. Berlin/New York: de Gruyter.

't Hart, J. (1986) Declination has not been defeated – A reply to Lieberman et al. *Journal of the Acoustical Society of America, 80*, 1838.

't Hart, J., Collier, R. & Cohen, A. (1990) *A Perceptual Study of Intonation: An Experimental Phonetic Approach*. Cambridge: Cambridge University Press.

Van Borsel, J., Janssens, L. & Santens, P. (2005) Foreign accent syndrome: An organic disorder? *Journal of Communication Disorders, 38*, 421–429.

Verhoeven, J., De Pauw, G. & Kloots, H. (2004) Speech rate in a pluricentric language: A comparison between Dutch in Belgium and the Netherlands. *Language and Speech, 47*, 299–310.

Verhoeven, J. (2005) Illustrations of the IPA: Belgian Dutch. *Journal of the International Phonetic Association, 35*, 243–247.

Verhoeven, J., Mariën, P., Engelborghs, S., D'Haenen, H., De Deyn, P.P. (2005) A foreign speech accent in a case of conversion disorder. *Behavioural Neurology, 16*, 225–232.

Wechsler, D. (1987) *Manual for the Wechsler Memory Scale – Revised*. New York: Psychological Corporation.

Wechsler, D. (1970) *Handleiding WAIS Nederlandstalige bewerking*. Lisse: Swets & Zeitlinger.

Wechsler, D. (1981) *Manual for the Wechsler Memory Scale – Revised*. New York: The Psychological Corporation.

Appendix 1 Transcription of Intonation Contours

In this transcription, the accented syllables are in bold. The pitch in each syllable is specified as follows:

1 = Promincence-lending rising pitch movement early in the syllable.

5 = Rising pitch movement preceding a prominence-lending fall rendering it more prominent.

2 = Non-prominence-lending continuation rise.

A = Prominence-lending falling pitch movement late in the syllable.

B = Falling pitch movement between syllables. This movement does not lend prominence, but it can be considered as a resetting of the pitch to the lower declination level.

E = Half fall.

& = Combines two movements on the same syllable.

0 = Low declination.

Ø = High declination.

Ik heb **twee we**ken ge**le**den een CV**A** gedaan en sinds**dien** ben ik ge**deel**tlijk ver**lamd**.
0 0 1&B Ø B 01 B 0 001 Ø B 0 0 1&B0 0 0 1 Ø Ø A
(Gloss: Two weeks ago I had a stroke and since then I have been partially paralyzed)

Da's gebeurd ja.
1 Ø A 0
(Gloss: That's what happened)

Nee, ik heb **niks ge**voeld.
1&A0 0 1 Ø A
(Gloss: No I didn't feel anything)

Ik **zat** op de WC   en ik **voel**de mij evens mij niet goed.
0 1&A0 0 0 1&B0 0 1 B 0 1 B 0 0 2
(Gloss: I was on the toilet and for a moment I didn't feel well)

Maar ik had **he**lemaal geen **pijn** en ik **viel zo naar rechts** …
0   0   0 1&A 0 0   0 1&B 0 0 1 E E   A
(Gloss: But it wasn't painful and I fell to the right)

En dan **la**ter ben ik op de **grond** gevallen
0   0 1 B 0 0 0   0 1&A 0 0 0
(Gloss: and later I fell to the ground)

En **toen heeft mijn man mij** gevonden
0   1   E   E   E   E   A
(Gloss: and then my husband found me)

Hij heeft toen een **dok**ter ge**beld**
0   0   0   0   1 B   0 1&B
(Gloss: He then called a doctor)

En **die** heeft dan de **ziek** enwagen besteld
0 1&B 0   0   0 1&A 0 0 0   0 0
(Gloss: and he then called an ambulance)

(Unintelligible) … en den **dok**ter nog …
                        0   0   1 Ø   Ø
(Gloss: … and the doctor …)

Enne … **die**   hebben mij **toen** (unintelligible)
0   0   1&B 0   0   0 1&B
(Gloss: and … they … have)

En dan euh … **is heb**ben ze mij **weg**gevoerd en … **ook** nog **zuur**stof gekregen.
0   0   0   1 1 Ø   Ø Ø   A 0 0   0   1   B 1 Ø Ø A 0
(Gloss: and then they took me away … and also got oxygen)

En **die**   hebben me **toen** naar **Her** entals gebracht
0 1&B 0   0   0 1&B 0 1&A 0 0   0 0
(Gloss: and they took me to Herentals)

En **daar** hebben ze dan een EKG gemaakt en een **scan**ner
0 1&B 0   0   0   0   0 0 0 1 Ø   Ø B 0 0   1 Ø B
(Gloss: and there they made an electrocardiogram and a scan)

En … en … euh **bloed** genomen en **dan**   ben ik naar de inten**sie**ve gegaan.
0   0   0   1   Ø Ø   B 0 1&A 0 0   0 0 0 0 1&A 0 0 0
(Gloss: and took blood and then I went to ER)

Na een **drie**tal dagen zo.
0   0   1&A 0   0   0   0
(Gloss: After about three days)

... **ik**   nog **kon** was **ja**   en **nee**
   1&B 0   1&B 0   1&B 0   1&B
(Gloss: I could only say yes and no)

Da'k een **vreemd** accent heb.
1&B 0   1   Ø A   0
(Gloss: that I have a strange accent)

zo op ... **op** zijn **Frans**
0 0   1   Ø   A
(Gloss: a French one)

Ja, ik **hoor** dat **ook** dat het **ans** ... **an**ders is dan **vroe**ger
0   0 1&B   0 1&B 0   0   1&B   1 Ø Ø   Ø   1   0
(Gloss: Yes I also hear that it is different from before)

Maar ik **weet** niet ... ik heb al ge**zegd** dat ik het de het **Grob**bendonkse ... dia**lect**
   0   0   1   B   0   0   0 01&B 0 0   0   0   0 1&A 0   0   0   0 1
(Gloss: but I don't know ... I have said that I still have to (learn) the dialect from Grobbendonk)

nog zal moeten leren **leren**
Ø   Ø   Ø Ø Ø Ø 5A 0
(Gloss: I will have to learn it)

Ja, ik **ken** het nog ... ik kan het **nu** niet zeggen nee.
0   0 1   Ø   B   0   0   0 1   Ø Ø   Ø   B
(Gloss: Yes, I still know it ... I can't say it now)

... **gaat** bijna **niet**.
    1   Ø Ø A
(Gloss: is almost impossible)

ja-nee wij spraken euh dit **di** – a – **lect**
0   0   0   0 0   0   0 1   Ø   A
(Gloss: Yes, no we spoke this dialect)

Chapter 6

A note on voice quality measurement in atypical prosody description and therapy

Evelyn Abberton, Honorary Senior Research Fellow, Department of Speech, Hearing and Phonetic Sciences, University College London

Adrian Fourcin, Emeritus Professor, University College London

Speakers with different impairments can have unusual prosody. These suprasegmental features have their origin in peripheral or central speech productive or perceptual processing, or in psycho-social difficulties. In all cases there is advantage in having access to accurate quantification. In this chapter we show how quantitative physical measurement with direct reference to vocal fold vibration can be matched to relevant aspects of speech production and perception, and provide visual patterns of pitch, loudness and phonation type in connected speech. These measurements and displays can supplement, and offer insights into, qualitative linguistic descriptions of prosody – and the elusive percept of 'tone of voice'. We show how the measures and real-time displays, directly related to production and perception, can be used for patterned bio-feedback in therapy and teaching, and contribute to evidence-based practice. The analyses and displays are produced using software running on a laptop, and both microphone and Laryngograph® (EGG) signals are used.

Voice quality and tone of voice

Voice quality is a prosodic feature of prime perceptual and communicative importance, contributing to speaker identification (Abberton & Fourcin, 1978), speech intelligibility, and a listener's assessment of the speaker's physical and mental health (Leff & Abberton, 1981). It is the focus of attention for clinicians and their dysphonic clients in Voice Clinics, and important for teachers and therapists working with hearing-impaired children and adults. Nevertheless, description and definition of normal and atypical perceived voice qualities are far from straightforward: labels are impressionistic, using multi-sensory terminology, and the physiological, acoustic and auditory features of a given voice quality often elusive, with complex inter-relationships between percept and quantitative physical characterization (Abberton, 2009).

The term 'voice quality' may be used to cover both laryngeal and vocal tract features such as nasality and articulatory settings, or may be restricted to laryngeal features, specifically mode of vocal fold vibration. A useful and manageable approach is to use the term for laryngeal features but not to restrict it to phonation type. Vocal fold vibration plays a key role in intelligibility as input to the vocal tract, and it is a rich source of emotional and personal information. However, a speaker's perceived voice quality depends also on pitch and loudness features: average pitch, pitch range and, of course, intonation. The subtle interactions between pitch and phonation type in conversation must also be taken into account. Voice quality, 'tone of voice', is essentially a feature of conversational connected speech. The social role of voice quality is recognized in Voice Clinics for dysphonic speakers in Quality of Life questionnaires such as the Voice Handicap Index (Jacobson, Johnson, Grywalski, Silbergleit, Jacobson, & Benninger., 1997).

Rationale for measurement: Quantitative aspects

Apart from the natural focus in Voice Clinics, voice quality as a concept and area of study and intervention has received much less attention in work with 'atypical' speakers than certain forms and functions of intonation. This is the case in foreign language teaching and learning, and in certain developmental and acquired pathological conditions (this volume). Informally, various impressionistic terms have been used such as dull, monotonous, singsong, over-precise, bizarre, but more analytic studies have focused, for example, on phonological features such as linguistic stress placement in an utterance and on inappropriate or dysfluent phrasing (McCann & Peppé, 2003), or on phonetic signals for turn-taking in a conversation (Kelly & Beeke, 2007).

A major concern of modern Phonetic Science is to relate different levels of description of speech. Appropriate physical (acoustic, physiological) measurements can illuminate the often complex relationships between different levels of representation. Rather abstract linguistic descriptors can be correlated with perceptual and productive parameters and measurements. Physical characterization of speech events is not only interesting and insightful but can also contribute to teaching and therapy planning by pinpointing difficulties and providing biofeedback, enabling the classroom and clinic to benefit from evidence-based practice.

The analysis and visual display of aspects of voice quality must not be simply a matter of number crunching and arithmetic convenience but should reflect human processing in terms of speech production and perception. This means, for example, that displays of fundamental frequency (the major correlate of perceived pitch) should be on a logarithmic, octave scale to reflect the way we hear pitch changes. Phonation type should be shown changing from cycle-to-cycle to correspond to the way the way the vocal folds vibrate and the way we perceive vocal smoothness or roughness. In this way, demonstration and bio-feedback of voice quality features can be appropriately patterned.

Examples for a normal speaker

The following figures illustrate these principles with examples of British English intonation from a woman.

Figure 1 is for the utterance "She can see him" with a falling nuclear tone on "see". In conventional orthography this contextually determined prominence

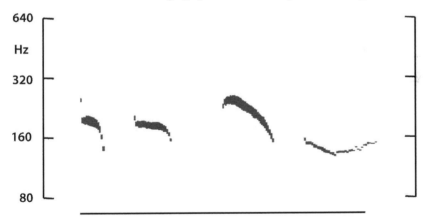

1 second

Figure 1 She can SEE him.
"Pitch" and "loudness" pattern with falling nuclear tone on "see". Note that these measurements are made from the instantaneous frequency and peak acoustic pressures in each vocal fold vibration cycle. In normal phonation, as here, these voice features are smoothly controlled.

could be indicated by capital letters, SEE, or italics *see*. Conventional intonation marking would be `see.

In the figure, the horizontal axis is time, and the vertical axis is logarithmic fundamental frequency, the major correlate of perceived pitch in speech. The traces are made up of points/dots, each one representing a cycle of vocal fold vibration with no smoothing or averaging. In this way, perceptually and linguistically relevant changes in pitch and phonation type are shown. The thickness of the trace is derived from the amplitude of the speech and relates to perceived loudness. Gaps in the traces relate to silence, or to voiceless consonants, [S] [k] [s] and [h] in this example.

Displays of this sort are obtained by combining electro-laryngography/ glottography and acoustic microphone recording. The laryngeal information is obtained from superficially applied electrodes, and the analyses and displays, based on the characteristics of auditory processing for speech (Fourcin, 2009; Fourcin & Abberton, 2007) are provided by the Speech Studio suite of analyses from Laryngograph Ltd.

Figure 2 shows 'pitch' and 'loudness' traces for the same sentence but with the falling nuclear tone on 'can'.

These two figures show clearly an important feature of English intonation, the contextually-determined placing of linguistic stress in an utterance. 'She can SEE him' answers the question 'What can she do?', whereas 'She CAN see

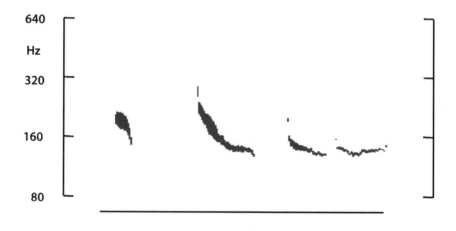

Figure 2 She CAN see him.
"Pitch" and "loudness" pattern with falling nuclear tone on "can".

him' either contradicts a previous statement 'She can't SEE him', or answers the question 'Can she SEE him?' Rule-governed nuclear placement is an essential but difficult aspect of English intonation for non-native speakers of English to control, and the feature of misaligned stress in pragmatic prosody can be particularly problematic in autism (McCann, Peppé, Gibbon, O'Hare & Rutherford, 2007).

Simple but perceptually and linguistically patterned real-time visual displays can offer a pedagogic or therapeutic tool for feedback which is not simply binary – 'right' or 'wrong' – but show speakers where and how they have made a mistake or succeeded. A structured sequence of exercises on nuclear placement can be used with deaf children, for example, or learners of English as a foreign or second language. Cavalli and Hartley (2010) illustrate the bio-feedback principle for a puberphonic speaker.

Figure 3 shows fundamental frequency, Fx ('pitch') and amplitude, Ax ('loudness') for the utterance 'She should TRY' with a falling nuclear tone. The common English feature of utterance-final creaky voice is shown by the broken trace at the end of the fall produced by cycles of vocal fold vibration of different durations.

In Figure 4, two more perceptually relevant features have been added: voiceless frication for sibilant consonants is represented by shaded blocks at

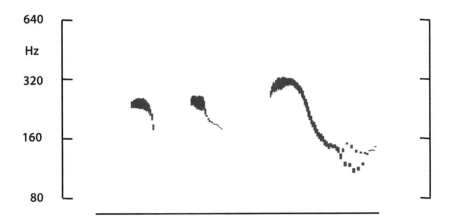

1 second

Figure 3 She should TRY.
"Pitch" and "loudness" pattern with nuclear tone on "try", and final creaky voice. Note that the use of cycle-by-cycle analysis had made it possible to represent the diplophonic character of the phonation.

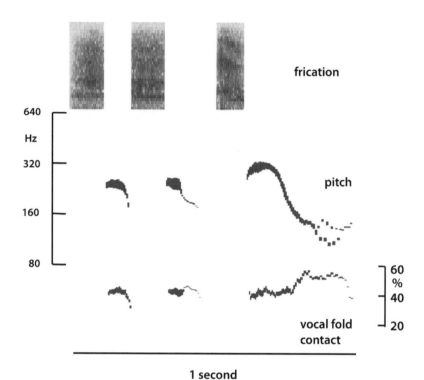

Figure 4 She should TRY.
"Pitch" and "loudness" pattern as in Figure 3 but also with patterned frication for each voiceless consonant. The lowest trace shows instantaneous contact phase for each cycle of vocal fold vibration, with thickness of the trace representing peak acoustic pressure for each cycle.

the top of the figure. The acoustic noise of the frication for these consonants is of the order of 5–6 KHz, but for visual integration of the visual patterns for the phonetic features shown to be congruent with the normal auditory integration of the high and low frequency components of speech, the frication patterns are placed just above the pitch and loudness traces. Once again, the feedback provided is not simply binary – frication present or absent – but patterned: for the two instances of the voiceless palato-alveolar fricative [S] the vowel context affects the structure of the frication, and for the voiceless affricate in 'try' the transition is evident.

The lowest trace in Figure 4 shows another basic aspect of voice quality – vocal fold contact quotient (Qx) modulated by amplitude/loudness. Perceived vocal roughness is often correlated with variability of the durations of vocal fold vibratory cycles, as in creaky voice. However, a voice can still sound rough even if there is no appreciable temporal variability as in creak (Fourcin & Ptok, 2003). Thus is due to variability in the duration of vocal fold contact quotients, even if the durations of successive complete cycles are regular. The relationship between Fx ('pitch') and Qx (vocal fold contact quotient) is often complementary for normal speakers, as seen in Figure 4: at higher pitches Qx is relatively short (around 40% here), and vocal fold contact duration is longer at lower pitches – around 50–60% at the end of the falling nuclear tone illustrated here. For the control of both pitch and phonation type the detailed cycle-by-cycle displays of the sort illustrated provide insight into productive difficulties at both the linguistic and physiological levels.

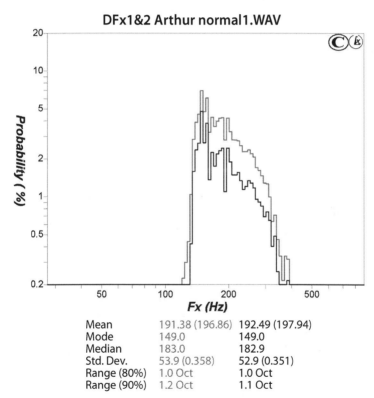

Mean	191.38 (196.86)	192.49 (197.94)
Mode	149.0	149.0
Median	183.0	182.9
Std. Dev.	53.9 (0.358)	52.9 (0.351)
Range (80%)	1.0 Oct	1.0 Oct
Range (90%)	1.2 Oct	1.1 Oct

Figure 5a Pitch range – normal.
Fundamental frequency range for the same speaker as in Figures 1 — 4, based on a two-minute recording. The outer distribution is based on the measurement of every individual vocal fold cycle. The inner distribution comes from only those occasions when two successive cycles are in the same analysis frequency bin. The similarity between the two distributions indicates that this speaker has smoothly changing pitch contours.

CFx Arthur normal1.WAV

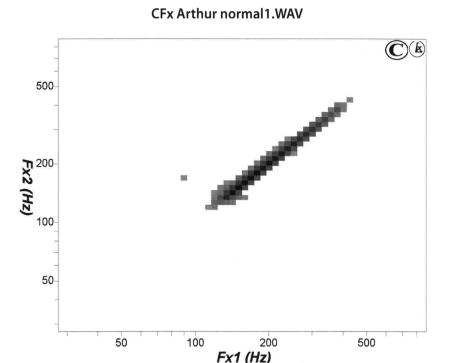

Figure 5b Pitch regularity (IF×3.25%).
Crossplot for the same speech sample based on successive vocal fold cycles. Irregularity of vibration (IFx) is the proportion of vocal fold cycles that fall outside the central diagonal.

Comparison with atypical prosodic use

Figures 5 and 6 contrast overall pitch use for a normal adult female speaker with analyses from a dysphonic woman.

Pitch range and its associated measures of central tendency are important indicators of gender and vocal health. Figure 5a shows the Fx ('pitch') range for approximately two minutes of fluently read speech. The outer distribution of values, DFx1, shows the analysis for every cycle of vocal fold vibration in the speech sample (some 10,000). The inner distribution, DFx2, is the second order distribution analyzing only those pairs of successive vocal fold vibrations that fall in the same perceptual and statistical bin. Because of intonational pitch changes the number of cycles analyzed is smaller than for the first order distribution but, for this normal speaker with a smooth voice, the general shape is the same for the two distributions, and the measured coherence reflecting this is high. The shape of the pitch range distribution is of indexical interest: probability of occurrence of particular fundamental frequencies is shown vertically, and it is clear that most of the pitch and intonation 'work' is being done in the lower part of the speaker's pitch range. Distributions of this shape seem to be typical for examples of speech of this length from adult female speakers. Male speakers tend to have more symmetrical normally distributed distributions. Leff and Abberton (1981) have shown how the shape of the pitch distribution in terms of skewness and kurtosis can help in diagnosis in mental health.

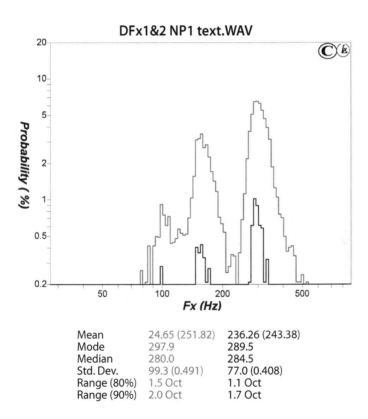

Mean	24.65 (251.82)	236.26 (243.38)
Mode	297.9	289.5
Median	280.0	284.5
Std. Dev.	99.3 (0.491)	77.0 (0.408)
Range (80%)	1.5 Oct	1.1 Oct
Range (90%)	2.0 Oct	1.7 Oct

Figure 6a Pitch range – abnormal.
Fundamental frequency distribution for a female speaker with scarred vocal folds (data courtesy of Julian McGlashan FRCS). Note the striking difference between the inner and outer distributions; this gives a simple and immediate indication of the intrinsic irregularity of this speaker's voice.

CFx NP1 text.WAV

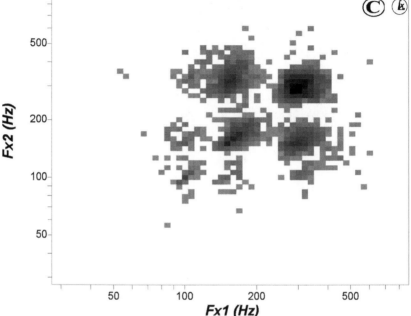

Figure 6b Pitch regularity - abnormal (IF×65%).
This crossplot shows the very great irregularity and extreme diplophonia of the speaker's voice in terms both of the spread of the individual lobes and their position away from the diagonal.

Regularity of vocal fold vibration, correlating with perceived vocal smoothness, is shown by the absence of discrete outlying peaks, and also in the CFx crossplot for the same speech sample in Figure 5b. In this analysis, the frequency of each vocal fold vibration is plotted against the value for the preceding vibratory cycle. The more regular the vocal fold vibration is during the pitch changes of intonation, the clearer the diagonal plot that emerges. For this speaker, the irregularity value, IFx, is only 3.25%, but values up to about 10% for women and 13% for men are normal (Ptok, Iven, Jessen & Schemmle, 2006), with children often having higher values.

Analyses of dysphonic speech

Figures 6a and 6b show the same analyses as in Figure 5 but for a dysphonic woman with vocal fold scarring.

Figure 6a shows that this speaker has an abnormally wide pitch range with three distinct peaked fundamental frequency distributions reflecting her diplophonic voice quality (alternating vocal fold cycles of different durations) and consequently distorted intonation contours. The inner, second order distributions, are very much smaller than the first order plots since she has temporally extremely irregular vocal fold vibration. This irregular fundamental frequency control is shown in the CFx crossplot in Figure 6b where, far from the clear diagonal obtained for a normal voice, widespread scatter can be seen with distinct lobes. The percentage irregularity, IFx, is 65%.

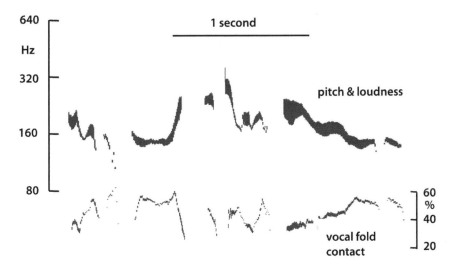

Figure 7 He wouldn't say "yes", and he wouldn't say "no" either.
The two traces show complementary aspects of control for a normal woman speaker. As in earlier figures, the upper trace combines the physical correlates of pitch and loudness, and the lower trace primarily shows the vocal fold contact percentage .

The effect of dysphonia on basic aspects of intonation

Figures 7 and 8 show the contributions of fundamental frequency, loudness, rhythm and phonation type to perceived voice quality for the normal female speaker in earlier figures and the female speaker with scarred vocal folds of Figures 6a and b. The displays are for the utterance 'He wouldn't say "Yes", and he wouldn't say "No", either', taken from a reading of the standard text 'Arthur the Rat'.

For the normal speaker, the utterance is probably best analyzed as having two intonation groups, the first ending with a rising nuclear tone on 'yes', and the second having a falling nuclear tone on 'no', with subsidiary falling pitch on 'either', making this word prominent in the tail. In the second intonation group, there is a falling head on 'wouldn't say', but any perceptual prominence marked by loudness (thickness of the trace) as well as pitch change occurs in the nuclear tone and tail. An alternative analysis would be to assign two intonation groups to the stretch 'and he wouldn't say "no", either', with a mid-level nuclear tone on 'no', and a low fall nuclear tone on 'either'. There is no pause, and voicing is continuous between these two groups. Other notable features are: the wide pitch range of about an octave (as would be expected since the speaker is a confident reader and experienced occupational voice user), and the regularity of vocal fold vibration evident in the smooth fundamental frequency contours. The broken fundamental frequency trace in the second syllable of the first occurrence of 'wouldn't' is due to the clear glottalization of [t] after the syllabic nasal at the lower end of the speaker's pitch range. The phonologically voiced intervocalic fricative in 'either' is seen to be phonetically only partially voiced, as is normal

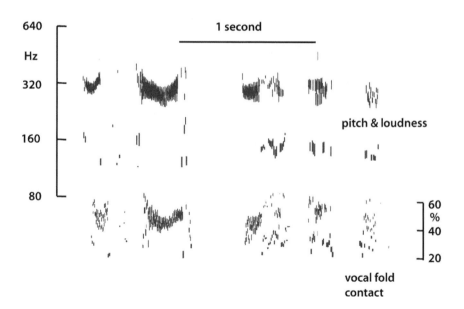

Figure 8 He wouldn't say "yes", and he wouldn't say "no" either.
The same utterance as in Figure 7 is now displayed for a pre-operative dysphonic woman speaker. There are clear visual correlates to the auditory roughness, in regard to pitch, loudness and vocal fold contact.

for intervocalic phonologically voiced obstruents. The perceived voice quality is 'clear', 'strong', well-controlled and appropriate for an adult woman.

As indicated earlier, for this normal speaker, fundamental frequency and vocal fold contact quotient (Qx) traces tend to be complementary. As fundamental frequency (pitch) increases, the values of Qx decrease. There are shorter vocal fold contacts at higher pitches, and longer contacts at lower pitches. The Qx contours are seen to be changing smoothly, but in the opposite direction to the fundamental frequency contours. There is a straightforward correlation between perception of the voice quality and the physical analyses, and their visual representation.

Figure 8 shows analyses and displays for the female speaker with scarred vocal folds producing the same utterance as the normal speaker. This utterance is most straightforwardly analyzed as having three intonation groups. The first has a rising nuclear tone on 'yes'. The second has a falling nuclear tone on 'no', and the third group, consisting of the single word 'either', also has a fall correctly placed on the first syllable. Linguistically, the intonation is normal, but the tone of voice is highly abnormal for an adult woman. The percept is of a hoarse, childish 'little

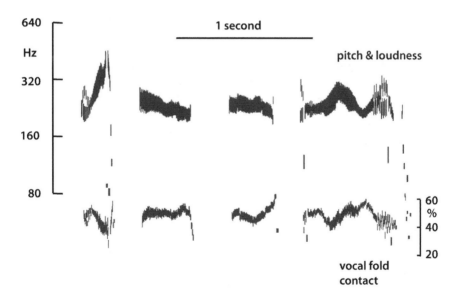

Figure 9 He wouldn't say "yes", and he wouldn't say "no" either.
The post-operative plots for the same utterance as in Figures 7 and 8 now show much improved temporal organisation and regularity, and the intonation contours are much clearer.

girl voice' and this correlates with the abnormally high fundamental frequency (pitch) and amplitude (loudness) traces at around 320Hz. The pitch range is extremely narrow as she is using only the upper values of her abnormally wide three-peaked fundamental frequency range, as shown in Figure 6a. Vocal fold vibration is perceptually rough and highly irregular as shown by the broken traces, with many outlying vocal fold cycles in the 'pitch' contours.

Figure 9 shows the major improvements that can be seen and heard after surgery to treat the vocal fold scarring.

The intonation patterns are linguistically the same but the pitch range has widened, and average pitch has lowered to an appropriate value. Vocal fold vibration is generally much more regular, although there is still irregularity at onset and offset of some voiced stretches. The perceived voice quality is brighter and clearer and obviously that of an adult woman.

For this dysphonic speaker, pre-operatively, vocal fold vibration was impaired both in terms of length of vocal fold cycles (Fx) and also vocal fold contact quotient (Qx). The perceptual roughness correlates with the extreme scattering of points seen in the Fx / Ax 'pitch' and 'loudness' traces and also in the vocal

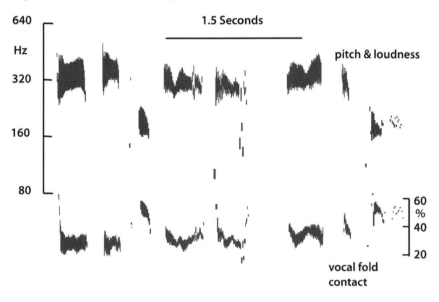

Figure 10 They made funny faces at each other, and raced each other.
Traces from a puberphonic speaker before visual feedback therapy by Lesley Cavalli. The two vocal registers, falsetto and modal, are clearly seen in the upper trace. Of particular note in the lower trace are the relatively small vocal fold contact values.

fold contact (Qx) trace. The complementary relationship between fundamental frequency and contact quotient values evident for the normal speaker is not seen for this impaired speaker. Post-operatively, perceptually the voice is much improved and this change is seen in the Fx / Ax traces which are more clearly organized, although still reflecting moments of roughness – particularly in the word 'either'. Qx is also changing much more smoothly with pitch changes, and (apart from 'either') there is also evidence of the fundamental frequency – Qx complementarity emerging.

Figure 10 shows traces for the puberphonic male speaker described by Cavalli and Hartley (2010). He is reading a story about a bus, and the utterance analyzed is 'They made funny faces at each other, and raced each other'.

In this example, the intonation patterning is obscure because of the two vocal registers the speaker is using: most of the time he is using falsetto at about 320 Hz, but his voice drops to the appropriate pitch and normal modal phonation type to indicate prominence on 'faces' – an atypical way to mark the location of a nuclear tone, before reverting to falsetto. In the second clause, 'other' at the end of a falling pitch sequence is also in modal voice.

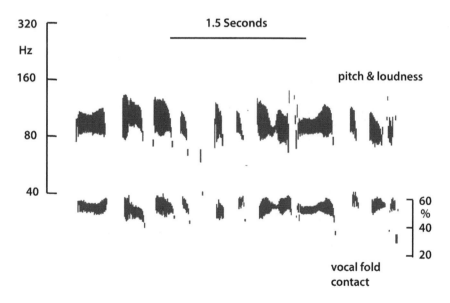

Figure 11 They made funny faces at each other, and raced each other.
The post-therapy traces for the speaker of Figure 10 now show coherent organisation with substantial lowering of average pitch and a large increase in vocal contact values.

After brief visual feedback (see Figure 11) work he can read (and speak spontaneously) in his normal appropriate low-pitched voice with no excursions into falsetto. His phonation type has changed from the falsetto register to normal modal. His average fundamental frequency is appropriately around 90Hz, although his pitch range is narrow – reflecting the fact that he is concentrating on reading.

The Qx values for contact quotient duration are striking for this speaker. Before therapy, the vocal folds are in contact for about 30% of each vibratory cycle during his high pitched falsetto phonation, but between 50 and 60% when modal phonation is used. After therapy Qx values are consistently between 50 and 60% correlating with the perception of a strong, loud, low pitched voice.

Conclusion

Atypical prosody can occur in speakers with impairments in peripheral or central speech production or perceptual processing, or with psycho-social difficulties. Deafness, dysphonia, motor speech disorders, genetic syndromes, stammering, autism, puberphonia, depression, gender dysphoria, can all have associated characteristic 'tones of voice'. Quantitative physical analysis may usefully supplement impressionistic and linguistic descriptions in defining speakers' difficulties. These analyses must relate to human processing, taking into account both auditory psychophysics and speech production. Mathematical processing by itself and not based on perceptual processing is insufficient. Relevant measures can be made of perceptually and linguistically important features to contribute to evidence-based practice, and real-time visual displays of pitch, loudness and phonation type can be used for patterned bio-feedback in therapy and teaching.

Acknowledgments

We are most grateful to Julian McGlashan FRCS, Lesley Cavalli MRCSLT and Ben Hartley FRCS for permission to use their pathological data. The figures have been produced using the Speech Studio hardware and software from Laryngograph Ltd, www.laryngograph.com.

References

Abberton, E. (2009) Don't look at me with that tone of voice! The Gunnar Rugheiner Lecture 2009. *Communicating Voice, 10:2,* 5–6.

Abberton, E. & Fourcin, A. (1978) Intonation and speaker identification. *Language and Speech, 21:4*, 305–318.

Cavalli, L. & Hartley, B. (2010) The clinical application of electrolaryngography in a tertiary children's hospital. *Logopedics Phoniatrics Vocology, 35: 2*, 60–67.

Fourcin, A. (2009) Aspects of voice irregularity measurement in connected speech. *Folia Phoniatrica et Logopaedica, 61:3*, 126–136.

Fourcin, A. & Abberton, E. (2007) Hearing and phonetic criteria in voice measurement: Clinical applications. *Logopedics Phoniatrics Vocology, 32*, 1–14.

Fourcin, A. & Ptok, M. (2003) Closing and opening phase variability in dysphonia. In: T. Wittenberg, G. Schade, F. Müller & M. Hess (Eds) *Advances in Quantitative Laryngology, Voice and Speech Research*. Stuttgart: Fraunhofer IRB Verlag.

Jacobson, B., Johnson, A., Grywalski, C., Silbergleit, A., Jacobson, G. & Benninger,M. (1997) The Voice Handicap Index: Development and Validation. *American Journal of Speech-Language Pathology, 6*, 66–70.

Kelly, D. and Beeke, S. (2007) Using Conversation Analysis to Assess and Treat Prosody in Autism. Paper presented at the Conference on Speech Prosody in Autism, University of Reading.

Leff, J. and Abberton, E. (1981) Voice pitch measurements in schizophrenia and depression. *Psychological Medicine, 11(4)*, 849–852.

McCann, J. and Peppé, S. (2003) Prosody in autism spectrum disorders: A critical review. *International Journal of Language and Communication Disorders, 38*, 325–350.

McCann, J., Peppé, S., Gibbon, F., O'Hare, A. and Rutherford, M. (2007) Prosody and its relationship to language in school-aged children with high-functioning autism. *International Journal of Language and Communication Disorders, 42:6*, 682–702.

Ptok, M., Iven, C., Jessen, M. and Schemmle, C. (2006) Objektiv Gemessene Stimmlippenschwingungsirregularitat vs Subjektiver Eindruck der Rauhigkeit. *Zeitschrift HNO, 54*, 132–136.

Chapter 7
Speech prosody in dysarthria

Gwen Van Nuffelen, Antwerp University Hospital

Prosody in dysarthria

Dysarthria is a speech disorder caused by disturbances in muscular control over the speech mechanism due to damage of the central or peripheral nervous system (Darley, Aronson & Brown, 1975; Duffy, 2005). It is characterized by slow, weak, imprecise and/or uncoordinated movements of the speech musculature (Yorkston, Beukelman, Strand & Bell, 1999). One of the best known etiologies is stroke, but dysarthria can be caused by a variety of divergent neurologic conditions such as traumatic brain injury, degenerative diseases (e.g., Amyotrophic Lateral Sclerosis and Parkinson's disease), inflammation, muscle diseases and demyelinating diseases (e.g., Multiple Sclerosis). Consequently, a considerable part of the population, elderly as well as youngsters, suffers from dysarthria.

As dysarthria disturbs the movement of speech musculature, it may affect one or more subsystems of speech, including prosody. Prosodic features in dysarthria depend upon the localization of the lesion (Duffy, 2005). In the late 1960s, researchers at the Mayo Clinic tried to distinguish, label and categorize the deviant speech characteristics occurring in dysarthria (Darley, Aronson & Brown, 1969a; Darley, Aronson & Brown, 1969b; Duffy, 2005). Their findings were based on perceptual analysis of a large group of individuals with dysarthria and, even today, their classification and their list with distinctive speech characteristics is still the gold standard for clinicians and researchers. Out of the 38 distinctive speech characteristics determined by Darley and colleagues 10 are related to prosody. The most common prosodic features are probably slow rate, monopitch, reduced stress and monoloudness. But dysarthric speech can also be characterized by, for example, increased speech rate and excessive stress and loudness variations. An overview of the most distinctive prosodic features per type of dysarthria is provided in Table 1.

Many of these perceptual prosodic characteristics, like monopitch in most types of dysarthria and excessive fundamental frequency shifts in ataxic

Table 1: Different types of dysarthria: associated lesion localizations and most deviant speech characteristics (Duffy, 2005; Duffy, 2007; Brookshire, 2007; Van Nuffelen, 2009-a).

type of dysarthria	lesion localization	prosodic features
spastic	UMN[b]: bilateral	slow rate*, short phrases, monopitch, monoloudness, reduced stress, excess & equal stress
UUMN[a]	UMN[b]: unilateral	slow rate
flaccid	LMN[c]	stridor/audible inspiration*, short phrases*, monoloudness, monopitch
ataxic	cerebellum	excess & equal stress*, excess loudness variations*, prolonged intervals, slow rate, monoloudness, monopitch
hypokinetic	basal ganglia	monopitch*, monoloudness*, reduced stress*, variable rate*, short rushes of speech*, inappropriate silences*, increased rate in segments*, increase of rate overall*
hyperkinetic	basal ganglia	inappropriate silences*, excess loudness variations*, audible inspirations*, alternating loudness*, monopitch, monoloudness, short phrases, prolonged intervals, reduced stress
mixed	two or more of above	combinations of above

a: Unilateral upper motor neuron, b: Upper motor neuron, c: Lower motor neuron, *: tend to be distinctive or more severely impaired than in any other single dysarthria type dysarthria, have been backed up by acoustic measurements (Kent & Rosenbek, 1982; Le Dorze, Ouellet & Ryalls, 1994). However, acoustic data for speech rate do not automatically match with the perception of rate. This will be further discussed below.

Prosody in dysarthria: Clinical relevance

Traditionally, clinicians often consider prosody, especially intonation, as the icing on the cake (Liss, 2007) – the finishing touch which is addressed after all other deviant speech characteristics are treated. However, recent publications teach us that prosody plays a major role when it comes to speech intelligibility – which in this context should be interpreted as the degree to which a listener understands the auditory signal produced by a speaker (Duffy, 2007) – and comprehensibility – defined as the extent to which a listener understands utterances produced by a speaker in a communication context (i.e., the knowledge shared by the speaker and listener on time, place, topic, purpose, intention, feelings associated with the message, and so on) (Barefoot, Bochner, Johnson & vom Eigen, 1993; Yorkston, Strand & Kennedy, 1996). De Bodt, Hernández-Díaiaz and Van de Heyning (2002) found that intelligibility in dysarthria can be described as a linear combination of the four main subsystems of speech, with articulation directly followed by prosody and with voice and resonance having a considerably smaller impact. One of the reasons that prosody has an important impact on speech intelligibility has to do with listeners' strategies to decode pathological speech. To understand a sentence or longer message produced by an individual with dysarthria, a listener first has to parse the continuous acoustic information into separate words (Liss, 2007). In the case of mildly to moderately impaired speech, listeners rely mainly on word recognition to define word boundaries. However, in severe dysarthria, word recognition becomes difficult and listeners have to look for another way to identify separate words. They will automatically start scanning the signal for cues such as, among others, pauses (related to speech rate) and syllabic strength contrasts. Speech rate also plays an important role when it comes to word recognition. On the one hand, decreasing articulation rate has been shown to enhance phoneme identification by increasing articulatory displacements, resulting in more perceptually and acoustically distinct phonemes (Tjaden & Wilding, 2004; Turner, Tjaden & Weismer, 1995). On the other hand, adding more pauses or elongating them provides the listener with more time to recognize a word correctly (Liss, 2007; Hammen, Yorkston & Minifie, 1994; Yorkston et al., 1999).

Prosody also affects a speaker's comprehensibility, partly through its effect on intelligibility, but also by its linguistic and paralinguistic functions. Peppé (2009) distinguishes two linguistic functions, the grammatical and the pragmatic function of prosody. There are three grammatical functions of prosody. Firstly, prosody provides the equivalent of written punctuation, indicating where sections of utterances, or phrases, begin and end. This contributes to word segmentation, but it also allows the listener to distinguish major from minor syntactic phrases and to recognize an enumeration. Secondly, prosody allows the listener to determine the type of phrase produced by the speaker. Did your communication partner just make a statement or did he ask a question? This is not unimportant if interlocutors wish to have an efficient conversation. A third grammatical function is the use of stress placement to distinguish word classes, e.g., noun and verb (e.g., (an) OBject – (to) obJECT). A speaker may also want to indicate focus by emphasizing a word or a word-group (e.g., 'MIKE goes to London', meaning that Mike goes and not someone else); this is the pragmatic function of prosody (Peppé, 2009). Individuals with dysarthria will often use this function when repeating an utterance which was primarily not completely understood by the listener (e.g., Patient: 'Tomorrow I leave for Antwerp.'; Speech therapist: 'When are you leaving and where are you going to?'; Patient: I leave TOMORROW for ANTWERP.'). Finally, affective prosody adds a non-linguistic meaning to an utterance by revealing the feelings and the attitude of a speaker regarding their utterance.

As improving intelligibility and, in extension, comprehensibility, is the primary goal of speech therapy (Weismer, Laures, Jeng, Kent & Kent, 2000; Theodoros & Thompson-Ward, 1998; McNeil & Kennedy, 1984), and as prosody clearly affects both entities in various ways, prosody should not be treated as an aside but, on the contrary, deserves the clinician's full attention in both assessment and treatment of individuals with dysarthria.

Assessment of prosodic skills

Assessment of intonation and stress-placement

There are commonly three ways to assess intonation and stress in clinical practice: overall perceptual judgement, transcription, or assessment of communicative functions of prosody.

Often, assessment of prosody is limited to an overall perceptual mapping of prosodic features. This gives the clinician a general idea of the patient's intonation and speech rate. Is the speech monotonous, characterized by monoloudness and monopitch or on the contrary by excessive and equal stress and excessive loudness variations? Is the patient's speech rate atypical and, if so, is it pathologically decreased or increased? Clinicians often have their own checklist for perceptual analysis of dysarthric speech but Darley et al.'s list of distinctive features (1975; published in Duffy, 2005) is widely used. The advantages of using a checklist to assess a patient's prosodic skills are multiple: it can be based on a conversational sample, it is not time consuming and it provides enough information for a clinician to decide whether or not these dimensions of speech are impaired and need treatment. However, such an analysis does not give any detailed information on intonation patterns and stress-placement. This information can be gathered through transcription, determining stress-placement, pitch patterns, speech rate and loudness variations.

There are several systems to transcribe prosody. The extended version of the IPA (Duckworth, Allen, Hardcastle & Ball, 1990) is intended to be suitable for transcription of pathological speech. In English, two assessments were published that evaluate expressive prosodic skills by means of transcription of a spontaneous speech sample: the Profiling of Prosody or PROP (Crystal, 1982) and the Prosody-Voice Screening Test or PVST (Shriberg, Kwiatkowski and Rasmussen, 1990). However, transcriptions are time-consuming; to be representative, the speech sample should be of a considerable length, so transcriptions are not very popular in clinical practice. Furthermore, information on prosody collected via a transcription of a conversational sample may be incomplete as the sample does not automatically convey different types of phrases, different stress-placements, intonation patterns, emotions and so on. Another point that clinicians should bear in mind when transcribing intonation and stress is that it is subjective and not reliable. Trials with groups of listeners show that pitch and loudness changes are not always perceived in the same way by different judges (Peppé, 2009). Therefore, transcriptions are preferably based on the data presented by a software program that visualizes the waveform and duration and acoustically analyzes intensity and fundamental frequency. PRAAT (free downloadable; Boersma and Weeninck, 2001) is one of the many programs that allows for such an analysis.

Thus, the suitability of prosodic transcriptions for clinical assessment of dysarthric speech seems to be limited due to the fact that it is time consuming and has doubtful reliability. There is, however, another even more important issue that questions the appropriateness of this method to assess a speaker's prosodic skills. As mentioned earlier, the main goal of speech therapy in individuals with dysarthria is to improve the patient's intelligibility and comprehensibility (Weismer et al., 2000; Theodoros & Thompson-Ward, 1998; McNeil & Kennedy, 1984). From this point of view, it is more relevant to know whether a speaker is able to transfer a specific meaning of an utterance conveyed by prosody than to know how that linguistic or paralinguistic function is achieved. Which prosodic changes are made is less important than whether the intended meaning is perceived by the listener. For example, if the patient is asked to emphasize 'Mike' in the sentence 'Mike goes to London', it actually doesn't matter whether focus is placed by means of pitch rise or by increased loudness and/or duration as long as the listener can hear the focus-placement, as this is important for interpreting the message. If desired, such an assessment can be extended by a perceptual or acoustic analysis to determine why prosody is deviant and inefficient.

A good starting point for assessing the communicative functions of prosody is the division in linguistic and paralinguistic functions as described earlier. Table 2 lists these functions and indicates their effect on intelligibility and comprehensibility. Peppé and McCann (2003) developed a test that allows the clinician to assess the communicative functions of prosody (see also Chapter 1, this volume). The test is currently already available in English, Spanish, French, Dutch and Norwegian. The author is not aware of another similar test but researchers of an inter-university project in Belgium called Computerized Assessment and Treatment of Rate, Intonation and Stress (Van Nuffelen, Martens, Dekens, Verhelst & De Bodt, 2009c) are currently working on a standardized speech technology-based assessment tool for prosodic functions in Dutch-speaking individuals with dysarthria.

Although dysarthria is a motor speech disorder that causes disturbed production of speech, it is recommended to assess the person's receptive prosodic skills. Speech therapy for intonation and stress is, as discussed below, often based upon auditory-perceptual feedback. Evidently, such therapy will not be effective if the patient's perception of prosody is disturbed. Today, receptive prosodic skill tasks are not a fixed part of the assessment of motor speech disorders. A review of the literature reveals, however, a couple of reasons why receptive prosody should be taken into account in individuals with impaired expressive prosody due to damage of the nervous system. A study by Orbelo, Grim, Talbott and Ross (2005) showed that the ability to comprehend affective prosody is impaired in the elderly and that this impairment could not be ascribed to peripheral hearing loss or cognitive functioning. They concluded that loss

Table 2: Impact of the different prosodic functions on intelligibility and comprehensibility

prosodic function	effect on intelligibility	effect on comprehensibility
grammatical functions		
• providing oral punctuations	identification of syntactic units/ word and sentence boundaries	distinct major from minor syntactic phrases and facilitates recognition of an enumeration
• discriminate between phrase types	facilitates word segmentation and recognition	interpretation of meaning
• stress-placement (syllabic strength contrasts)	facilitates word recognition and segmentation	interpretation of meaning
• pragmatic function: focus placement	-	interpretation of meaning
• affective prosody	-	feelings and the attitude of a speaker regarding his utterance

of comprehension of affective prosody in the elderly is due to an aging-related impairment of the right hemisphere. This is clinically relevant, as the majority of patients with dysarthria are elderly. Another argument to assess receptive prosody in dysarthria is the location of brain areas associated with reception and comprehension of prosody. Whereas receptive emotional prosody is located in the left temporal region (Mitchell, Elliot, Barry, Cruttenden & Woodruff, 2003; Wildgruber, et al., 2005; Peppé, 2009), reception of linguistic prosody is localized in the left frontal region (Wildgruber, Hertrich, Riecker, Erb et al., 2004; Peppé, 2009). Thus, there is a strong possibility that receptive prosody is impaired in individuals with dysarthria, especially in those with unilateral upper motor neuron dysarthria or spastic dysarthria. But since knowledge of receptive prosody in motor speech disorders – with or without associated disorders like aphasia or cognitive disorders – is lacking, it is recommended to assess the patient's receptive prosodic skills independently of the type or etiology of dysarthria. The PEPS-C (Peppé & McCann, 2003) can be used for this purpose.

Assessment of speech rate

In accordance with assessment of intonation and stress clinicians often make an overall perceptual judgement of speech rate. Often this perceptual analysis is limited to placing the speaker's rate into one of the following three categories: decreased, normal or increased speech rate. A more detailed analysis can be made by means of the speech rate-related distinctive features of Darley and colleagues (Darley et al., 1969a; Darley et al., 1969b; Duffy, 2005).

Another method to assess speech rate is by calculating the speaker's speaking rate (SR) and articulation rate (AR). Both measures are expressed as the number of syllables produced per second, but whereas pauses are included in the time measure for SR, they are excluded for determination of AR (Van Nuffelen, De Bodt, Wuyts & Van de Heyning, 2009b). Traditionally, calculating SR and AR is done manually. The clinician or researcher determines the number of syllables produced by the patient, the duration of the complete utterance and, in order to determine AR, also the total duration of silent pauses. Generally, a pause is considered to be a silence when it has duration of at least 200 ms (Turner et al., 1995). Measures of SR and AR are preferably based on spontaneous speech productions. However, in the case of moderately and severely impaired speech, reading passages make it easier to determinate the number of syllables produced by the patient, and working with a firm text limits the time spent in counting syllables. Clinicians may also be interested in a patient's SR and AR during reading as they often use reading material in their exercises. However, they should keep in mind that speech rate measures may differ depending on the task. Currently, there is no consensus in the literature concerning the impact of a task on SR and AR in both non-impaired and impaired speech (see, among others, Fitzsimons, Sheahan & Stauton, 2001; Kent, Kent, Rosenbek, Vorperian & Weisner, 1997). A recent study (Vanvooren, Van Nuffelen & De Bodt, 2007), in which we investigated AR and SR for both reading and spontaneous speech in 30 individuals with dysarthria and a control group of 25 individuals without any speech impairment, showed a significant difference between both tasks for both AR and SR in both groups (p<0.001). Speaking rate was in both groups found to be significantly lower during spontaneous speech compared to reading. However, the task effect on AR differed between groups. For the control group the effect was in accordance with the effect for speaking rate, meaning that the articulation rate was lower during spontaneous speech compared to reading. The opposite was found in the dysarthric group. This issue obviously requires further research, but it is recommended that SR and AR for reading and SR and AR for spontaneous speech be approached as two different measures.

Clinicians who often calculate a patient's SR and/or AR, and compare these with control data, may sometimes find a discrepancy between the measures and their perceptual impression of speech rate. Ziegler, Hoole, Hartmann and von Cramon (1988) did not find a correlation between perception and measures of speech rate in dysarthric speakers with perceptually increased speech rate. Turner and Weismer (1993) found the same result in three individuals with Amyotrophic Lateral Sclerosis (ALS). Verwaeren, De Bodt and Van Nuffelen (2007) found normal or even reduced SR and/or AR in individuals with various types of dysarthria whose speech rate was perceptually judged to be increased. It is therefore recommended to not restrict the clinical assessment of speech rate to an overall auditory-perceptual judgement.

Calculation of AR and SR is, however, obviously time consuming. A partial solution for this is *Tally*, a software program developed by Yorkston, Beukelman and Tice (1988). The Tally program is designed to automatically measure speaking rate, not articulation rate. As the program knows the number of words and syllables of the used text fragment, speaking rate can easily be calculated. SR measures based on the automatic function of the Tally are probably not always one hundred percent accurate as the program does not take into account syllables and words that are added or omitted by the speaker (e.g., reading errors, spontaneous reaction) but they can always be adjusted by the clinician.

Obviously it would be interesting to have an objective, automated assessment of speech rate. In recent decades, the use of acoustic measurements for speech evaluations have gradually increased. In the case of voice assessments, acoustic analyses in particular are an established part of clinical assessment world-wide (Baken & Orlikoff, 2000; Holmberg, Ihre & Södersten, 2007; Schneider, Zumtobel, Prettenhofer, Aïchstill & Jocher, 2010). However, there are very few clinical tests available that allow acoustic analysis of speech rate. The Motor Speech Profile (Kay Pentax®) automatically calculates a speaker's diadochokinetic rate (i.e., the ability of a speaker to quickly and accurately produce a series of rapid, alternating sounds). The author is not familiar with any other program that provides automated measures of SR or AR for normal or pathological speech. However, the prospects for the future are promising. Researchers have established algorithms that are capable of tracking reliable SR and AR data from non-impaired speech samples (Dekens, Demol, Verelst & Verhoeve, 2007) and this knowledge is currently being used to develop algorithms that allow determination of speech rate in dysarthria (Van Nuffelen et al., 2009c).

Prosody as a part of therapy

Treatment of intonation and stress

Techniques of intervention

As discussed previously in the paragraphs on assessment of intonation and stress, reception of prosody is important when it comes to treatment of impaired expressive prosody as therapy is often based on modelling and auditory-perceptual feedback. Thus, to maximize the effect of intervention techniques targeting expressive prosody, improving receptive prosodic skills might be the first step in treatment. Furthermore, Peppé, McCann, Gibbon, O'Hare, and Rutherford (2007) found that receptive and expressive prosody skills were significantly correlated, not only in the experimental group (children with high-functioning autism) but also in their control group. As mentioned previously, they advocate that expressive problems may be improved by intervention based on receptive skills. This certainly requires further research.

Two techniques with which clinicians are well familiar are behavioral instructions (e.g., 'Raise your pitch at the end of the sentence', or 'Increase your intensity on that syllable') and modelling ('I'm going to produce a sentence with a specific intonation pattern. Please repeat this sentence and try to copy the pattern'). Both techniques require good patient receptive skills. If the patient can not identify success and failure, the clinician can function as a reference, thereby improving and refining the patient's judgements. This can be combined with audio-recordings, allowing the patient to listen again to his own utterance.

Another technique to improve expressive prosody is visual feedback. Displaying fundamental frequency, intensity, duration of words and phrases and pauses may help the patient to produce the required stress or intonation pattern. Some support for this comes from a study by Caligiuri and Murry (1983) in which three individuals with dysarthria were able to improve their prosody by means of oscilloscopic feedback about intensity, duration and intra-oral pressure.

Content of intervention

The content of intervention depends upon which aspects or functions of prosody are impaired. The most common exercises are listed below:

1 *Chunk utterances into natural syntactic units.* When inhalation or pausing does not occur at natural syntactic boundaries, this will disturb the intonation and stress pattern and the naturalness of speech. Patients are taught to inhale or pause at logical syntactic boundaries within their limited breath group.

2 *Extend breath groups.* The duration of syntactic units/breath groups in speech varies from 2 to 8 seconds (Duffy, 2005). Due to their physiological limitations, individuals with dysarthria often have shorter breath groups that do not match with the syntactic units. Clinicians can try to improve the patient's breath control in order to extend the breath groups.

3 *Contrastive stress tasks* (phrases/words in which the segmental information does not vary but the stress patterns do) can be used to improve three prosodic functions: 1) stress-placement to distinguish word-classes (e.g., (a) 'REcord' versus (to) 'reCORD'); 2) stress placement to emphasize a word or word-group (e.g. 'MIKE goes to London' versus 'Mike goes to LONDON'); and 3) to distinguish between types of phrases (e.g., 'Ann likes fruit' versus 'Ann likes fruit?').

4 *Affective prosody.* The patient can be asked to produce the same sentence with different feelings and emotions.

In 2007, Yorkston et al. published a systematic review of evidence for the effectiveness of treatment of loudness, rate or prosody (i.e., suprasegmental aspects of speech that extend across a series of sound segments, including stress patterning, intonation, and rate-rhythm) in dysarthria. The authors concluded that, because of the relatively small number of studies, most of which are case studies, and the heterogeneity of treatment techniques and participants, few conclusions about treatment effectiveness can be drawn. However, there is, as described in the paragraph on clinical relevance, a rationale for making prosody a part of therapy in dysarthria. It is hoped that guidelines for treatment of prosody in dysarthria will follow from future research.

Treatment of speech rate

Speech rate is considered to be an important aspect of speech therapy in dysarthria, but not in the way that people who are unfamiliar with dysarthria would expect (namely normalization of speech rate). It seems utterly logical for therapists to help patients decrease speech rate in instances of habitually high rates and to increase speech rate in individuals with pathologically low rates. However, although it may help speech to be more natural-sounding (Dagenais, Brown & Moore, 2006), the latter is not common practice (Yorkston et al., 2007) as it generally does not improve speech intelligibility. Rate reduction or rate control, on the other hand, is believed to have the power to improve speech intelligibility in dysarthria. Speech rate can be slowed down by either decreasing articulation rate, inserting more (appropriate) pauses or increasing pause duration (Figure 1). Increasing articulation time is believed to improve articulatory precision and coordination. This theory has been confirmed by a number of studies. The results of a study by Turner et al. (1995) in individuals with dysarthria secondary to ALS suggested an expansion of the vowel acoustic working space (i.e., the area described by vertical and horizontal tongue movements in order to produce distinct vowels) and higher acoustic-perceptual distinctiveness as rate was slowed, and Tjaden and Wilding (2004) found that rate reduction increases articulatory displacements, resulting in more distinct phonetic events. By enhancing phoneme identification and thus facilitating the listener's perceptual processes (i.e., word recognition and segmentation), improved articulatory accuracy may result in increased intelligibility (Figure 1). Also adding extra pauses or increasing pause duration may positively affect the listener's perceptual decoding strategies (Figure 1) by producing more appropriate breath group units, resulting in recognizable syntactic units, by clearly indicating word-boundaries (e.g., pacing) or simply by providing the listener more time to decode the produced signal (Yorkston et al., 1999; Hammen et al, 1994; Liss, 2007).

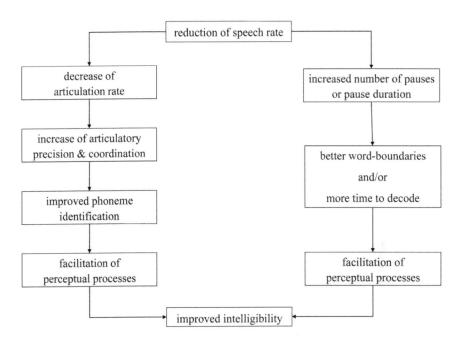

Figure 1: How rate reduction may improve speech intelligibility

Methods for rate control

To slow down a patient's speech, a clinician can choose from a variety of techniques, as follows.

Speaking slower on demand is a flexible rate control method that respects the natural prosodic pattern. The patient is instructed to reduce his/her rate to a certain percentage of his/her habitual rate, e.g., 'speak half as fast as you are used to' (Yorkston and Beukelman, 1981; Tjaden and Wilding, 2004; Turner et al., 1995).

Pacing is another frequently-used method for rate control. There are several devices that can be applied to pace a patient's speech: a pacing board, a metronome and, more up-to-date, the program *Pacer* developed by Yorkston et al. (1988). A pacing board is a board divided into separate squares or slots. The patient is asked to indicate one square per word or syllable (Duffy, 2005). Of course, a simple metronome can be used but the *Facilitator of Metronomic Pacing* (Kay Elemetrics) allows the clinician to

Table 3: The effect of the investigated RCMs on articulation rate, total pause duration, mean pause duration and number of pauses of various rate control methods (Van Nuffelen et al., 2010).

method	articulation rate	total pause duration	mean pause duration	pause frequency
demand				
alphabet board	↓*	↑*	↑*	↓°
pacing board	↓*	↑*		↑°
hand tapping	↓*			↑°
DAF50	↓*			
DAF100	↓*			
DAF150	↓*			

*p<.001; °p<.05; ↓ : decrease; ↑ : increase

select the desired rate (clicks per minute) and provides visual feedback. Another advantage of the *Facilitator of Metronomic Pacing* is that it can be worn as a portable device. The software program, *Pacer*, paces the patient's speech by underlining, highlighting, putting in bold or adding words one by one at a rate determined by the speech therapist. It can be used with every sentence, paragraph or text (Yorkston et al., 1988).

Using an *alphabet board,* the patient points to the first letter of each uttered word (Duffy, 2005). If the listener can also see the board, this method not only improves intelligibility and consequently comprehensibility by slowing down speech rate, but also by providing a visual cue to the listener which will facilitate word recognition (Hustad and Garcia, 2005).

Another method to reduce speech rate is *hand* or *finger tapping*. Applying this method, the speaker taps once per uttered syllable (Duffy, 2005), providing the listener with well-defined syllable boundaries.

Delayed auditory feedback (DAF) is a prosthetic rate control method. A DAF device generally delays the speaker's auditory feedback by between 50 and 200 milliseconds (Adams, 1997; Downie, Low and Lindsay, 1981; Hanson and Metter, 1980). A trial session gives the clinician and patient the opportunity to select the ideal delay.

Effect of various rate control methods on speech characteristics and intelligibility

When reading the descriptions of the different rate control methods, one may intuitively feel that these methods do not all affect SR and AR in the same way. Generally, the literature reveals little information on these aspects and, whenever data is available, it is usually limited to speaking rate (among others Hanson and Metter, 1980; Rousseau and Watts, 2002; Le Dorze, Dionne, Ryals, Julien and Ouelette, 1992). However, speaking rate depends on articulation rate and on the number of pauses and the pause duration. Van Nuffelen, De Bodt, Vanderwegen, Van de Heyning and Wuyts (2010) investigated the effect of various rate control techniques on SR, AR, total pause duration, mean pause duration and pause frequency. Table 3 (duplicated from van Nuffelen et al., 2010) presents the results of this study, confirming that the effect on speech varies across rate control methods.

The effects of rate control on speech provide a rationale for reducing speech rate to improve intelligibility in dysarthria, independently of the habitual speech rate. However, research data reveal that rate reduction does not always improve the intelligibility of dysarthric speech. The results of previously-published studies on rate control in dysarthria vary from a significant positive effect (among others Le Dorze, 1992; Hustad & Sassano, 2002; Yorkston, Hammen, Beukelman, & Traynor, 1990), to no effect (among others Hammen et al., 1994; Dagenais et al., 2006; Tjaden & Wilding, 2004) to even a negative effect (Rousseau & Watts, 2002) on speech intelligibility. Comparison of the data (Van Nuffelen et al., 2009a) suggests that some therapeutic methods may be more effective than others, i.e., pacing and, to a lesser extent, DAF. However, it was only recently that the first studies comparing the effects of various rate control methods on intelligibility were published (Van Nuffelen et al., 2009b; Van Nuffelen et al., 2010). The results of their extended study (Van Nuffelen et al., 2010), based on 29 participants diagnosed with dysarthria and a running speech intelligibility below 90 percent (mean intelligibility: 62%), showed that the most effective methods were hand tapping, and using the pacing board and the alphabet board. Each of the investigated methods had the power to significantly improve speech intelligibility in at least one participant, but Van Nuffelen and colleagues also found that rate control often results in even more decreased speech intelligibility. Based on the current knowledge, the authors recommend judging the effect of rate control for a specific individual with dysarthria during a trial session, and trying out different methods and different rates. Where speaking more slowly on demand effectively improves the patient's intelligibility, it is the preferred method as it is the most natural one.

Acknowledgement

The author would like to acknowledge her colleagues Heidi Martens, Cindy Guns, Floris Wuyts and Paul van de Heyning and the engineers Tomas Dekens and Werner Verhelst for their intellectual input and their contributions to the research on prosody performed at the Rehabilitation Center for Communication Disorders of the Antwerp University Hospital, Belgium. A special word of thankfulness goes to Marc De Bodt, the Head of the Rehabilitation Center, who stimulated my interest in motor speech disorders and who has been an excellent guide through the years.

References

Adams, S.G. (1997) Hypokinetic dysarthria in Parkinson's disease. In M.R. McNeil (Ed.) *Clinical Management of Sensorimotor Speech Disorders* (pp. 261–286). New York: Thieme Medical Publishers.

Baken, R.J. & Orlikoff, R.F. (2000) *Clinical Measurement of Speech and Voice*, 2nd ed. San Diego, CA: Singular.

Barefoot, S.M., Bochner, J.H., Johnson, B.A. & vom Eigen, B.A. (1993) Rating deaf speakers' comprehensibility: An exploratory investigation. *American Journal of Speech-Language Pathology, 2(3)*, 31–35.

Boersma, P. & Weeninck, D. (2009) *PRAAT: Doing phonetics by computer (Version 5.1.05)* [Computer program]. Retrieved May 1, 2009, from http://www.praat.org/

Brookshire, R.H. (2007) *Introduction to Neurogenic Communication Disorders.* St. Louis, Misssouri: Elsevier Mosby.

Caligiuri, M.P. & Murry, T. (1983) The use of visual feedback to enhance prosodic control in dysarthria. In W. Berry (Ed) *Clinical Dysarthria* (pp. 267–282), Austin, Tx: Pro-Ed.

Crystal, D. (1982) *Profiling Linguistic Disability.* London: Edward Arnold.

Dagenais, P.A., Brown, G.R. & Moore, R.E. (2006). Speech rate depends upon intelligibility and acceptability of dysarthric speech. *Clinical Linguistics and Phonetics, 20 (2/3)*, 141–148.

Darley, F.L., Aronson, A.E. & Brown, J.R.(1969a). Differential diagnostic patterns of dysarthria. *Journal of Speech and Hearing Research, 12*, 246–269.

Darley, F.L., Aronson, A.E. & Brown, J.R. (1969b) Clusters of deviant speech dimensions in the dysarthrias. *Journal of Speech and Hearing Research, 12*, 462–496.

Darley, F.L., Aronson, A.E. & Brown, J.R. (1975) *Motor Speech Disorders.* Philadelphia: WB Saunders.

De Bodt, M. S., Hernandez-Diaz, H. M., & Van de Heyning, P. H. (2002). Intelligibility as a linear combination of dimensions of dysarthric speech. *Journal of Communication Disorders, 35*, 283–292.

Dekens, T., Demol, M., Verhelst, W., & Verhoeve, P. (2007, August) A comparative study of speech rate estimation techniques. *Interspeech* 2007, Antwerp, Belgium.

Downie, A.W., Low, J.M., Lindsay, D.D. (1981) Speech disorders in parkinsonism – usefulness of delayed auditory feedback in selected cases. *British Journal of Disorders in Communication, 16*, 135–139.

Duckworth, M., Allen, G., Hardcastle, W. & Ball, M.J. (1990) Extensions to the International Phonetic Alphabet for the transcription of atypical speech. *Clinical Linguistics and Phonetics, 4*, 273–280.

Duffy, J.R. (2005) *Motor Speech Disorders.* St. Louis, Missouri: Elsevier Mosby.

Duffy, J.R. (2007) History, current practice, and future trends and goals. In G. Weismer (Ed.) *Motor Speech Disorders* (pp. 7–56). San Diego, CA: Plural Publishing.

Fitzisimons, M., Sheahan, N. & Staunton, H. (2001) Gender and the integration of acoustic dimensions of prosody: Implications for clinical studies. *Brain and Language, 78*, 94–108.

Hammen, V.L., Yorkston, K.M. & Minifie, F.D. (1994) Effects of temporal alternations on speech intelligibility in parkinsonian dysarthria. *Journal of Speech Hearing and Research, 37*, 244–253.

Hanson, W.R. & Metter, E.J. (1980) DAF as instrumental treatment for dysarthria in progressive supranuclear palsy: a case report. *Journal of Speech and Hearing Disorders, 45*, 268–276.

Holmberg, E.B., Ihre, E. & Södersten, M. (2007) Phonetograms as a tool in the voice clinic: changes across voice therapy for patients with vocal fatigue. *Logopedics Phoniatrics Vocology, 32(3)*, 113–127.

Hustad, K.C. & Sassano, K. (2002) Effects of rate reduction on severe spastic dysarthria in cerebral palsy. *Journal of medical Speech-Language Pathology, 10*, 287–292.

Hustad, K.C. & Garcia, J.M. (2005) Aided and unaided speech supplementation strategies: Effect of alphabet cues and iconic hand gestures on dysarthric speech. *Journal of Speech Language and Hearing Research, 48(5)*, 996–1012.

Kent, R.D., Kent, J.F., Rosenbek, J.C., Vorperian, H.K. & Weismer, G. (1997) A speaking task analysis of the dysarthria in cerebellar disease. *Folia Phoniatrica et Logopaedica, 49*, 63–82.

Le Dorze, G., Dionne, L., Ryalls, J., Julien, M. & Ouelette, L. (1992) The effects of speech and language therapy for a case of dysarthria associated with Parkinson's disease. *European Journal of Disorders of Communication, 27,* 313–324.

Le Dorze, G., Ouellet, L. & Ryalls, J. (1994) Intonation and speech rate in dysarthric speech. *Journal of Communication Disorders, 27,* 1–18.

Liss, J. (2007) The role of speech perception in motor speech disorders. In G. Weismer (Ed.) *Motor Speech Disorders* (pp. 187–219). San Diego, CA: Plural Publishing.

McNeil, M.R. & Kennedy, J.G. (1984) Measuring the effects of treatment for dysarthria: knowing when to change or terminate. *Seminars in Speech and Language, 5,* 337–357.

Mitchell, R.L.C., Elliot, R., Barry, M., Cruttenden, A. & Woodruff, P.W.R. (2003) The neural response to emotional prosody, as revealed by functional magnetic resonance imaging. *Neuropsychologica, 41,* 1410–1421.

Orbelo, D.M., Grim, M.A., Talbott, R.E. & Ross, E.D. (2005) Impaired comprehension of affective prosody in elderly subjects is not predicted by age-related hearing loss or age-related cognitive decline. *Journal of Geriatric Psychiatry and Neurology, 18,* 25–32.

Peppé, S. (2011, this volume) Assessment of prosodic ability in atypical populations, with special reference to high functioning autism. In V. Stojanovik & J. Setter (Eds), *Speech Prosody in Atypical Populations: Assessment and remediation.* Guildford: J&R Press Ltd.

Peppé, S. & McCann, J. (2003) Assessing intonation and prosody in children with atypical language development: The PEPS-C test and the revised version. *Clinical Linguistics and Phonetics, 17,* 345–354.

Peppé, S., McCann, J., Gibbon, F., O'Hare, A. & Rutherford, M. (2007) Receptive and expressive prosodic ability in children with high-functioning autism. *Journal of Speech, Language and Hearing Research, 50,* 1015–1028.

Peppé, S.J.E. (2009) Why is prosody in speech-language pathology so difficult? *International Journal of Speech-Language Pathology, 11(4),* 258–271.

Rousseau, B. & Watts, C.R. (2002) Susceptibility of speakers with Parkinson disease to delayed feedback. *Journal of Medical Speech-Language Pathology, 10,* 41–49.

Schneider, B., Zumtobel, M., Prettenhofer, W., Aichstill, B. & Jocher, W. (2010)

Normative voice range profiles in vocally trained and untrained children aged between 7 and 10 years. *Journal of Voice, 24(2),* 153–160.

Shriberg, L.D., Kwiatkowski, J. & Rasmussen, C. (1990) *The Prosody-Voice Screening Profile.* Tucson, AZ: Communication Skill Builders.

Theodoros, D.G. & Thompson-Ward, E.C. (1998) Treatment of dysarthria. In B.E. Murdoch (Ed.) *Dysarthria: A Physiological Approach to Assessment and Treatment* (pp. 130–175). Cheltenham: Stanley Thornes.

Tjaden, K. & Wilding, G.E. (2004) Rate and loudness manipulations in dysarthria: Acoustic and perceptual findings. *Journal of Speech, Language and Hearing Research, 47,* 766–783.

Turner, G.S. & Weismer, G. (1993) Characteristics of speaking rate in dysarthria associated with Amyotrophic Lateral Sclerosis. *Journal of Speech and Hearing Research, 36(6),* 1134–1144.

Turner, G.S., Tjaden, K. & Weismer, G. (1995) The influence of speaking rate on vowel space and speech intelligibility for individuals with amyotrophic lateral sclerosis. *Journal of Speech and Hearing Research, 38,* 1001–1013.

Vanvooren, J., Van Nuffelen, G. & De Bodt, M. (2007). Spreeksnelheid en articulatiesnelheid bij normale sprekers en dysartriepatiënten: correlatie tussen lezen en spontane spraak en relevantie voor onderzoek en therapie [Speaking rate and articulation rate in normal speakers and patients with dysarthria: correlation between reading and spontaneous speech and it's relevance for assessment and treatment.]. Unpublished Master's thesis, Ghent University, Belgium.

Verwaeren, E., Van Nuffelen, G., & De Bodt, M. (2007). Correlatie tussen het akoestisch en perceptueel spreektempo bij dysartriepatiënten [Correlation between acoustic and perceptual speech rate in patients with dysarthria]. Unpublished Master's thesis, Ghent University, Belgium.

Van Nuffelen, G. (2009a) Speech intelligibility in dysarthria: Assessment and treatment. Doctoral dissertation, University of Antwerp, Belgium.

Van Nuffelen, G., De Bodt, M., Wuyts, F. & Van de Heyning, P. (2009b) The effect of rate control on speech rate and intelligibility of dysarthric speech. *Folia Phoniatrica et Logopaedica, 61,* 69–75.

Van Nuffelen, G., Martens, H., Dekens, T., Verhelst, W. & De Bodt, M. (2009c) CATRIS: Project overview. Retrieved 15 May 2010 from http://catris.etro.vub. ac.be/overview.html.

Van Nuffelen, G., De Bodt, M., Vanderwegen, J., Van de Heyning, P. & Wuyts, F. (2010) Effect of rate control on speech production and intelligibility in dysarthria. *Folia Phoniatrica et Logopaedica, 62,* 110–119.

Weismer, G., Laures, J.S., Jeng, J.Y., Kent, R.D. & Kent, J.F. (2000) Effect of speaking rate manipulations on acoustic and perceptual aspects of the dysarthria in amyotrophic lateral sclerosis. *Folia Phoniatrica et Logopaedica, 52,* 201–219.

Wildgruber, D., Hertrich, I., Riecker, A., Erb, M., Anders, S., Grodd, W. & Ackermann, H. (2004) Distinct frontal regions subserve evaluation of linguistic and emotional aspects of speech intonation. *Cerebral Cortex, 14,* 1384–1389.

Wildgruber, D., Riecker, A., Hertrich, I., Erb, M., Grodd, W., Ethofer, T., & Ackermann, H. (2005. Identification of emotional intonation evaluated by fMRI. *NeuroImage, 24,* 1233–1241.

Yorkston, K.M, & Beukelman, D.R. (1981) Ataxic dysarthria: Treatment sequences based on intelligibility and prosodic considerations. *Journal of Speech and Hearing Disorders, 46,* 398–404.

Yorkston, K., Beukelman, D. & Tice, R. (1988) PACER/TALLY. Communication Skill Builders. Tuscon,AZ. Communication Skill Builders.

Yorkston, K., Hammen, V.L., Beukelman, D.R. & Traynor, D.C. (1990) The effect of rate control on the intelligibility and naturalness of dysarthric speech. *Journal of Speech and Hearing Disorders, 55,* 550–560.

Yorkston, K.M., Strand, E.A. & Kennedy, M.R.T. (1996) Comprehensibility of dysarthric speech: Implications for assessment and treatment planning. *American Journal of Speech-Language Pathology, 5,* 55–66.

Yorkston, K.M., Beukelman, D.R., Strand, E.A. & Bell, K. (1999) *Management of Motor Speech Disorders in Children and Adults.* Austin, TX: Pro-Ed.

Yorkston, K.M., Hakel, M., Beukelman, D.R. & Fager, S. (2008) Evidence for effectiveness of treatment of loudness, rate, or prosody in dysarthria: a systematic review. *Journal of Medical Speech-Language Pathology, 15(2),* 11–36.

Ziegler, W., Hoole, P., Hartmann, E. & von Cramon, D. (1998) Accelerated speech in dysarthria after acquired brain injury: Acoustic correlates. *British Journal of Disorders of Communication, 23,* 215–228.

Index